5k, Ballet, and a

Spinal Cord Injury

By

Jennifer Starzec

and

Sarah Todd Hammer

Dedicated To:

YOU, because we KNOW that you have made it through hard times before, too!

A Note from the Authors

To all those with Transverse Myelitis-

We wish you the best in your recovery. Stay strong, work hard, and stay positive because we know you can do it! We don't know, and will probably never know, why certain people are faced with the challenge of Transverse Myelitis. All we know is that it takes a strong, determined person to beat it. Fight through the pain, fight through the tears, fight through the fear, and throughout it keep a beautiful smile on your face. YOU are as much of an inspiration to US as everyone else.

Love,

The authors, Sarah Todd and Jennifer

Table of Contents

Part 1: The Beginning

Part 2: Life with TM

Part 3: A Growing Friendship

Part
1
The Beginning

Sarah Todd

Everyone has adventures in their lives. Some good ones, some bad ones. I had a big one that started when I was eight years old, and is still affecting me today! It all started when I hopped off the bus after school on April 19th, 2010. My mom was at the bus stop waiting for me, and when I arrived we walked back to my house. I sat my backpack down before racing to the kitchen to grab vanilla ice cream from the freezer and chocolate syrup from the fridge. My mom fixed my snack and handed it to me, so I brought it over to the family room and sat down at the game table to eat it while watching TV.

My spoon clattered to the table, interrupting what I was doing. I had accidentally dropped it, and a thought occurred to me.

"Wouldn't it be horrible if I couldn't hold a spoon?"

I picked it back up and quickly finished my ice cream before going upstairs to my room where I would get ready for my ballet class.

After pulling on my leotard and tights and having my mom put my hair into a bun, I went downstairs, grabbed my dance bag, and hopped in the car with my mom to head over to my ballet class.

We pulled into the parking lot of the dance studio after about twenty minutes of driving. I got out of the car and walked into the studio. Little did I know that this wasn't going to be a normal ballet class.

"If you do not hope, you will not find what is beyond your hopes"
-St. Clement of Alexandria

Jennifer

"Fourth place? That's all? You have got to be kidding me!" I whined, looking at my age group results. I sat down on a worn-out wooden bench, the warm summer air surrounding me as I thought about the race. It wasn't the place that bothered me- fourth place was really good- but I wanted a medal. Jealousy took over as I realized that one of my best friends got third, and I was right next to her almost the whole time. I did some thinking. Maybe if I'd been training all summer, like last year, I could have done much better.

It's early August, 2011, and shortly after the last 5k race before the event that changed my life. Of course, I didn't know about this yet. All I cared about was my race, and how I had fallen behind my friend and her little brother right at the end of it.

"Look! Tom O'Hara is signing bibs!"
I got in line, bib ready for the former Olympic runner to sign, my solemn mood barely changed.

"What's your name?" Mr. O'Hara asked cheerfully a few minutes later, when I got up in front of him.

"Jennifer," I replied. He smiled.

"Well, that's a pretty name! Here you go!"
Mr. O'Hara handed back my number, a short message written on the side. I smiled as I read it, feeling a little bit better.

Sarah Todd

I was an ordinary eight-year-old girl. I loved the color pink, make-up, sparkly things and, most importantly, ballet.

I walked in the Dancer's Studio Backstage for my ballet class in Roswell, Georgia, wanting to sign up for the Atlanta Dance Theatre Ballet Company.

I walked into the classroom noticing that we were trying on our recital costumes. I was so excited! I quickly put mine on and danced around the room with my friend, Amanda. I was leaping and skipping around the room when I started to get a small headache on the back of my neck. It didn't hurt too much, but I told my teacher, Mrs. Jonnie. She said I'd be fine, so I continued to flutter across the room in my costume.

Soon, though, my headache got really bad, to the point that I was crying! I told Mrs. Jonnie, who went to get my mom, while my friends came over to me to see if I was okay. While they were looking at me, they noticed that the back of my neck was getting red.

Meanwhile, my mom peeked into the classroom window and noticed my friends gathered around me. She thought they were admiring my new hair clips until she saw that I was crying. She ran in to get me so she could bring me home to lie in bed.

My mom helped me take my costume off and I sat on the bench to put my pants and flip flops on. I noticed my tights were sagging, so I started to pull them back up. Then I noticed my hands slowing down, and then my arms, too! Suddenly they just collapsed.

"I can't move my arms!"

"Oh, God," she said. "We're not going home!"

Jennifer

The summer of 2011 was just packed with events. June was lazy, in a good way, but late July and pretty much all of August were very eventful. During those months I stayed at my cousin's house in the city for a couple nights, went on a camping trip with my family, and went camping with my church, amongst other things. Two days after the closing of my church camp-out was the biggest event of my life.

I woke up the morning of August sixteenth, 2011 to the sun shining through my windows. As I sat up I turned my head to the side, but immediately straightened it again when I felt a sharp pain shoot through my neck. Sure I had just slept on it funny, I tried to ignore it, and headed downstairs to eat breakfast.

After breakfast, I relaxed on the couch and saw that my mom was gathering her things for work. She asked me to help her find her shoes, but my neck was still stiff and hurting. I told her that, and that I couldn't help, which I'm sure annoyed her greatly, but she left me alone and found them herself.

What was this pain? It was strange, but I told myself to stop being so sensitive. It would wear off soon, and I'd be fine. At least that's what I thought.

> "Fall 7 times, stand up 8"
>
> -Japanese Proverb

Sarah Todd

My mom rushed me out to the car, and I walked with her. We went in the car, and I told her that I couldn't buckle myself. She did it for me. We were in the car to go to the urgent care facility for around twelve minutes. While we were in the car, my mom called my dad and explained where we were going.

Finally, we arrived. Knowing that only minutes earlier I had walked to the car, my mom picked me up out of the car and stood me up in the parking lot. My legs collapsed. I could still move them, but I couldn't walk.

My mom picked me up and carried me over to the building. Of course, I was eight years old and scared, and had no idea what was going on, so I was crying. My mom brought me over to the lady and, because she was scared as well, started practically yelling at her!

"Her name is Sarah Todd Hammer, and she can't move her arms!"

The lady immediately brought us to a room, where we saw a doctor, who decided that whatever was going on was beyond what he could do and had equipment for. He explained that we would have to go by helicopter to a bigger hospital. I was scared to be going on a helicopter and did not know what was coming for me next.

Jennifer

My neck still hurt, but not as much. An hour or so later I was back on my feet.

I wandered into the kitchen and decided to cook something to distract myself a little bit. I wasn't hungry, so I gave my creation to my brothers. They ate it right up, just as I'd predicted. Trust me, little boys will eat anything!

Finally, I decided it was time to get dressed. I wasn't going to let myself stay in my pjs forever, even though it was summer, as much as I really wanted to! So I walked back up to my room and searched through my clean clothes. Nothing, or at least nothing I wanted to wear. I went over to the laundry room to check in the dryer. I saw just the outfit I had been searching for, so I reached in to grab it.

"OW!"

As I stretched my arms out to grab my clothes, a horrible, searing pain shot up through my arms, neck and shoulders. It hurt so bad I forgot about getting changed and ran back downstairs to tell my dad. He told me to lie on the couch and rest, so I did.

But it never stopped. I was on the couch, tossing and turning. I thought it was the worst thing I had ever felt in my life! The intense, burning pain would come in spurts, too. Bad, a little better, worse, a teeny bit better, the absolute worst, almost no pain, complete agony.... And so on. During this I thought my left hand felt kind of funny. I shook my fingers out then studied my hand as I opened and closed it... Slowly?

Sarah Todd

I landed at the new hospital and was immediately sent to a room. I saw another doctor there. All he did that night was give me Motrin for my pain!

I was at that hospital for six hours listening to my parents plead for the doctor to run some sort of test. They were also throwing different diagnoses out at him.

"Is she having a stroke? Does she have a brain tumor? Does she have MS?"

However, the doctor didn't do anything. He thought I was faking it.

Finally, I was sent home. Just sent home!

"If she's not significantly better in the morning, then come back," he said.

"There are far, far better things ahead than any we leave behind."

–C.S. Lewis

Jennifer

"Dad, I think my left hand is getting weak!"

Of course, my dad didn't really believe me. Not that I blamed him. I was pretty sure I was just imagining things, anyway.

Unsatisfied with the couch, I went upstairs to watch TV. Nothing changed, although now I noticed that my lungs felt weird. Tight, like someone was squeezing them. I went back to my dad, who suggested a hot bath. When I told him about the odd tightness around my ribs, he told me not to add bubbles and to tell him if I needed anything.

So I filled the bathtub up, then lied down in it. It was warm and comfortable, and my shoulders didn't hurt as bad when I was in it. Finally, I decided the bath was long enough, and went back to my TV.

Overall, the relief I got from the bath didn't last. I sat on my bed, lied frontwards on my bed, lied backwards on my bed, on my stomach, on my side, on my back. Nothing worked. This blazing pain seemed to only be getting worse.

I heard the phone ring downstairs, then my dad answer it. I heard his footsteps climbing up the stairs over to the direction of my room.

"It's Mom. She wants to talk to you," my dad said, handing me the phone. I answered it, and my mom asked me if I needed to go to the hospital.

"I don't know," I said, fighting back tears. What if I said 'yes', and the doctors couldn't find anything wrong? What if I was over-exaggerating the pain, weakness, and weird sensations? I tried to explain this to her, deciding that I didn't need to go to the hospital. I handed the phone back to my dad.

But It just kept getting worse and worse to the point that I had to ask my dad to make me another bath. I got in it again, but this time the hot water made no difference. Because of this, I quickly got back out, absentmindedly realizing that I couldn't lift myself with my left hand, only my right. My right arm felt much, much stronger.

I started to redress. I got everything on except for my shorts. I started pulling them up with my right hand, now sure that my left wasn't working correctly. All of a sudden, my entire right arm went completely limp, and I could no longer pull my shorts up. I tried to move my right hand, move anything on it. There was nothing. I tried my left. My elbow was working, but I couldn't grasp onto the shorts to get them up more than they already were. All of a sudden, my right hand was dead, unplugged, and my left was definitely not working right.

"DADDY!"

"The secret of successes in life is for a man to be ready for his opportunity when it comes"

-Earl of Beaconsfield

Sarah Todd

After another twenty-five minutes in the car, we arrived home. My dad carried me to my house, my eyes filled with dried tears. We went inside the door to see my two brothers, John and Alex, and my grandma, Katie. Alex stood right at the door, and my grandma in the living room. John was standing next to Alex.

"What are you doing home?!" Katie said. That was the first thing that came out of anybody's mouth.

My parents told her everything that had happened. After the explaining, it was around 11:45 at night, so my dad carried me up to my room, with Mom, Katie, Alex and John following us. At this point I was tired and afraid, and my mind was everywhere.

When we arrived at my bedroom, I was set into my bed and Alex stood right by it.

He said, "So she can't walk? Or move her arms?" My mom nodded.

My mom slept with me that night. I kept having to ask her to scratch my arms, legs, or head if they got itchy. Even the littlest things were now a challenge, one I didn't understand.

Jennifer

A blur. That's what it felt like to me. My dad called my mom back, and they both decided that I definitely needed a hospital now. As my mom drove home to get me, my dad asked me to move different fingers on my right hand. But I couldn't.

One moment I was in the car, needing my mom to buckle my seat belt for me. The next I was in the emergency waiting room.

"Her shoulders have been hurting really bad and she can't move her right arm at all," my mom said to the ER lady. She looked down at me. Fatigue had started to set in right before my mom had picked me up to go to the hospital, and now my eyes showed it as I struggled to keep them open. My limp right arm was resting on my left, which I was holding tight against my body to keep from letting them dangle painfully. The lady told us to find somewhere to sit down.

The emergency room was annoyingly crowded, but I didn't think about it much. I slumped down in the chair and rested my eyes.

Shortly after, I was in a room, on a nice, comfy bed. Well, comfy to me, anyway since I was so exhausted. Later, I realized that the lady must have known something serious was going on, because I was let into a room before anyone else in the filled ER waiting room.

The doctor walked in. I wondered if there was anything he could do to make the pain disappear and my arms work again. I wondered if I was going to get any worse than I already was. If so, I wondered if he could fix that, too.

Sarah Todd

I woke up the next morning in my bed, happy because the doctor had said I would be better in the morning. I tried to move. Nothing. I was as still as can be. I looked to my right, noticing that my mom had left my bed and room. She probably couldn't sleep very well that night, after all that had happened. Surprisingly, other than the constant itchiness, I had slept pretty well!

Anyway, at this point I was freaking out! My legs and feet, which had both been able to move the night before, couldn't now.

"MOM!" I yelled, knowing my mom was probably downstairs. She was, and quickly made it up to my room. When she got there, she asked me to move a bunch of things.

"Lift your leg, scratch your head, wiggle your fingers; your toes..."

Nothing. Nothing at all.

Jennifer

The doctor asked lots and lots of questions. They were exhausting, but I answered them as best I could.

"When did the pain start? What did it feel like? How bad was it, on a scale of 1-10? Did you have any pain yesterday? How have you been feeling lately? When did you realize you couldn't move your arms? Was it sudden or gradual?"

I tried to remember the day's events, walking him through my story to fill the questions.

"Is her voice always like that?" He asked my mom, and I realized that my words were very slurred. My mom said no, but I was very tired so that was probably why.

"I am very tired," I slurred, still struggling to keep my eyes open.

"You can go to sleep, if you want," the doctor said to me.

"I can't," I responded, looking up at him. "I'm afraid to."

"Why? What are you afraid of?" He asked, eyes shining with genuine concern.

"I'm afraid that I'll stop breathing. My lungs feel... different."

The doctor nodded, then talked to my mom a little longer as I tried to concentrate on the TV. I caught bits and pieces of the conversation, but wasn't paying much attention.

"Bigger hospital.... Transport.... Ambulance...."

Sarah Todd

My mom quickly decided that she would call an ambulance to return to the hospital. Of course, I didn't want to go back to that horrible place. I wanted to stay home.

The ambulance arrived pretty fast, and before I knew it, five men were in my room, trying to get me onto a stretcher. They carried me on the stretcher down the stairs and onto the ambulance.

My dad drove his car alongside the ambulance. My mom rode with me in the back. We drove on the highway in major traffic, but the people driving the ambulance didn't bother to put their sirens on! My mom asked how long it would take to get to the hospital like that, and the driver said it would be about an hour. So, knowing it would take only twenty-five minutes or so without the traffic, my mom suggested that they turn the sirens on. Luckily, they did.

Before I knew it, I was racing across the highway in the ambulance. For the first time in my life, I didn't know what to think.

Jennifer

I had to be transported, transported to a bigger hospital with more specialists and more equipment. The doctor also wanted one with a PICU (Pediatric Intensive Care Unit) in case my breathing got any worse. My mom and the doctor discussed the different hospitals in the area, narrowing it down to two. Finally, that got narrowed down to one.

Before being transported, though, he decided to run a few tests, including a CT scan and blood work.

A bunch of paramedics soon burst into the room wheeling a gurney. They helped me out of bed, and I wobbled over to the gurney, nearly falling over. I didn't really think anything of the wobbly walking, though. After all, I was very tired and had been lying in bed for awhile.

I lied down on the gurney, and the paramedics put stickers all over my stomach and chest to monitor my heart and breathing. When they finished, they covered me with a blanket to keep me warm and put straps around me to keep me attached to the gurney.

All I saw were the ceiling lights flashing by as I was wheeled through the hospital into a large garage-like thing that held a bunch of ambulances. They slid me into one, hooked my stickers up to some machines and slammed the back doors. My mom nervously sat alongside the driver in the front. Two medics stayed with me in the back, but I barely acknowledged them. Everything just felt so surreal.

Before I knew it, I was once again being whisked down the hallways at the new hospital into an even bigger room, one that, unbeknownst to me, would be my home for what would feel like a long, long time.

Sarah Todd

I finally arrived at the hospital. Luckily, this time I was put in a room with an amazing doctor.

I had to do so many tests, including a huge MRI and a spinal tap.

During the MRI, I wasn't sedated. I had to be awake the whole time, and wasn't allowed to move at all during it! This didn't really matter much to me, though, because the only part of my body I could move at that time was my head and neck.

The spinal tap wasn't all that bad, either. I had lost all feeling, too, so I didn't feel a thing. I was really glad about that, because I've heard that spinal taps hurt really bad!

By the end of the day, I was exhausted. I was moved into the PICU, which held a bed, a bathroom and shower, a TV, a chair, a desk, and tons of medical wires! At this point, my breathing wasn't very great, even though it wasn't bad enough to get me hooked up to a vent, which was why I was living in the PICU.

That first day was rough. I had an awful pain in the left side of my neck that felt like someone was jabbing a huge knife into it! That ended up happening a lot in those days in the PICU. Of course, I also had all of those tests done, and hadn't eaten all day because of the MRI, so I was extremely hungry! My stomach was growling constantly, but I wasn't allowed to eat. I would have to live on IV food for a few more days.

The longest month and a half of my life was going to be spent in this place. The doctors came in saying they thought they knew my diagnosis. I was afraid to know.

Jennifer

I couldn't walk. This was my realization as I tried walking from the gurney to my new bed. I took a couple super wobbly steps, and the nurses had to catch me. I could move my legs, and they were fairly strong while I was lying down, but I couldn't walk. I couldn't stand or sit up on my own, either.

I guess I was a little delusional at this point, because I seriously did not think staying at the hospital even one night was an option.

Meanwhile, two different doctors pulled my mom out into the hall and told her that they felt I was faking whatever was going on.

I wasn't, of course, and also didn't know what was going on. Luckily, my mom knew that, too, and told those doctors that.

Then we got what most people, including myself now, would view as the good news, seeing the condition I was in, but was thought of as bad news to me then: I had to stay in the hospital overnight.

By the time the room was dark and empty of everyone but my mom and I, it was late, but hard to sleep, even though I was so tired....

I woke up. It was morning. Where was I? Oh, yeah. The hospital. You would think I would have known that since I had awoken to nurses checking my vitals!

A doctor came in. He pulled my mom out to the hall to explain to her that he thought whatever was going on was neurological, a myelitis of some sort. Within my earshot, he explained how I would probably need to stay at least another week. I thought that that was an insane amount of time for something that was probably not that big of a deal! I guess I was lucky that he didn't tell me that he was planning on keeping me much, much longer than that. However, what continued to go through my head was, "A week? At this place?"

He also mentioned that I would also need a huge brain and spine MRI soon.

I felt like I needed to say something. What was I going to say? As if on cue, my stomach growled.

"Can I eat breakfast? I'm hungry!"

The doctor looked a little uneasy, wondering if eating was actually a good idea. But since he probably didn't know when any of my tests would be, or what all of them were, he figured we'd try it for now.

So, he and my mom called 'room service'. Well, that is if 'room service' is defined by people bringing you food and has nothing to do with the quality of the food itself!

"The only way of finding the limits of the possible is going beyond them into the impossible"

-Arthur C. Clarke

Sarah Todd

The doctors said I had "Transverse Myelitis". Of course, I had never heard of that, and had no idea what it was!

Because of this, I had to be put on steroids. A couple days later, they were still not doing anything.

On April twenty-first, a doctor came in saying that I would have to have a surgery to have a port put in my right hip so I could have a plasmapheresis done. I was scared out of my mind, and so was my mom.

"I don't know if I want her to have surgery!" My mom told the doctor.

"You have to do this!" The doctor told us, "She won't get better any other way!"

Finally, my mom agreed, and later that day I was in surgery.

Jennifer

If you have never eaten eggs and potatoes while almost completely paralyzed from the neck down, you have never experienced "hard". Seriously.

Of course, my mom offered to feed me. I didn't let her, though, even though I couldn't move my right arm or hand at all, and my left only a teeny bit at the wrist and elbow. I hooked my limp left hand around the fork, and most of what was on my plate ended up on my lap, but I was determined to do everything myself that I possibly could do myself.

I was also at a point where everything felt like a dream, and I really did not know what was going on. I kept telling everyone who called that I felt fine, and exclaimed to my mom, "Why do people sound so concerned when they talk to me? I feel fine! I mean, I'm not dying!"

It's true. I wasn't dying. And I did feel fine, except for the paralysis and random bursts of pain. Plus, I thought I would be perfectly normal in just a matter of days. Or maybe even hours.

But I was acting a bit naïve. Not that I could help it. No one knew exactly what was happening to me. They wouldn't know until the MRI a couple days later, which is a whole story on its own.

"Nothing great was ever achieved without enthusiasm"

-Ralph Waldo Emerson

Sarah Todd

I finally woke up, out of surgery, and in the PICU. I felt safe back there.

Both of my parents were right in front of my bed, saying, "Sarah Todd... Are you awake?"

I was awake, but didn't respond because the anesthesia hadn't worn off completely yet.

That day I had my first plasmapheresis done. A big machine was used to clean out my blood and give me new plasma.

I continue to thank whoever the very kind person was that donated their plasma. Of course, I don't know who that person is. All I know is that they donated their plasma to Red Cross, and I now have it.

The plasmapheresis was a real life-saver, because later that day I moved my right big toe! It was just up and down, but of course everyone threw a party! I kept moving it over and over. It was a miracle.

Jennifer

On the day of the MRI, some of my family's closest friends, who are also our neighbors, came to visit. One of them French braided my hair, and we all talked. It wasn't until late that it was actually time for the MRI, and they all left as my mom and I went over to start it.

A lady greeted us and immediately got me onto the MRI bed after hooking my IV up to something. She started to pop some plastic over me, and one went on my face.

"Um, this is making me feel a little claustrophobic," I said to her nervously. I never would have cared much before, but for some reason my senses were heightened now, and the littlest things made me feel uncomfortable. It was definitely weird, and different, but that was the definition of my life since August 16th.

"WHAT DO YOU MEAN CLAUSTROPHOBIC? HOW DO YOU KNOW YOU'RE CLAUSTROPHOBIC?" She practically screamed.

I felt like crying.

As she was saying that, I was shoved into the MRI. It was going to be four hours long, which meant a long night.

"It is idle to dread what you cannot avoid"

-Publius Syrus

Sarah Todd

The next day, April twenty-third, I was finally allowed to eat! The only things I was allowed to eat were chicken broth, Jell-O, and Popsicles, but, surprisingly, I loved it.

I also continued to gain more foot and leg movement. The funny thing is, it seemed as if I got more movement whenever my mom left the room and left me with my dad!

"I need to leave more often!" she joked.

I had five days of plasmapheresis. It helped me so much! If I hadn't had that done, I wouldn't have gotten better. At all.

After twelve days in the PICU I was able to move to the rehab unit, where I would be for the rest of my hospital stay. There, I did therapy all day Monday through Friday!

I had an occupational therapist and a physical therapist. Luckily, I never needed speech therapy.

My OT worked on my shoulders a lot. She had me push my arms across a table many times as an exercise.

My PT made me some bright pink splints to wear on my legs as I was walking. She said they were to help keep my balance and my knees straight, and they did. I was still in a wheelchair for the most part, though, even though I was working on walking. By now, I could move my legs completely, although they weren't very strong.

Soon, though, I could walk from my bed to the wheelchair! I now had a pair of "grippy socks" to wear that supposedly stuck to the floor to keep me from falling.

But I had already fallen. Fallen into this deep dark hole. I was trapped. Trapped in this nightmare.

Jennifer

I felt as if the MRI would never be over. The only noise was the hammering of the machine, and I hurt all over. My head hurt from my braids and the hard head rest I was lying on. My legs ached from being in the same position for so long, and my arms were just hanging, so I was far from comfortable.

I had to move. There wasn't much I actually could move, but if I repositioned, say, my left foot or neck a little I felt slightly more comfortable... I mean, I knew the instructions. I knew that I wasn't supposed to move even my little toe. But I had to. I was more uncomfortable than I ever had been in my life.

"Jennifer! Stop moving!"

That's what I heard from the MRI lady every couple minutes. From time to time she also took me out of the machine to put straps over my legs, which didn't help at all.

Finally, she took me out of it completely.

"You're going to have to wait until another time, when you can sedate her," the lady rudely said to my mom. My mom explained how we had waited for a while for this MRI, and it was the middle of the night already.

We went to the bathroom after that for a break. My mom took out my braids. She didn't yet understand what I had and how uncomfortable I had been with the later-learned nerve pains, so she just reminded me that I had to be still through the whole MRI. I knew that already, but just couldn't stand what was beyond discomfort. Even now, I can't go more than three minutes without moving my legs and arms and getting into different positions, and it was even worse then, because I didn't understand what was going on at all.

When we got out of the bathroom, that lady was done with her shift. A man took her place, one that was beyond nice to us! I really liked him.

"First, let's get into this other machine. It's a little faster than the one you were in."

There was a faster one? I was pleasantly surprised. Was he just saying that to help me feel more at ease? I will never know, but it doesn't matter, because it worked.

The man put me on the new MRI bed. He put a lot of rolled up towels and blankets underneath my legs, arms, and head. He also put big headphones on me and allowed me to listen to music, something that the other lady had not mentioned.

The best part, though, were the breaks. He let me know how long I would have to be in there on each shift, and let me come out, breathe, and let my mom help reposition my arms and legs in-between. I was out in no time, all because of that nice man. What would I have done if I'd been stuck with Ms. Rude the whole time?

"What chance gathers she easily scatters. A great person attracts great people and knows how to hold them together"

-Johann Wolfgang Von Goeth

Sarah Todd

At the rehab unit they had a gym for therapy. I rode a really big, fun bike almost every time there! I loved it! A lot of the time, like when I rode that bike, therapy was fun. Other times, it was horrible.

One day during OT my therapist had me lying on my back on a big therapy ball. She had me try to sit up. The first few times I tried, it didn't work. Finally, on one of my tries, I did it! I sat up! I got tired after just that one, though.

At first, I could only sit up on the ball. Eventually, after working on it on the ball, I could sit up on a mat and in my bed! I was happy about that, of course!

Another day, I made another huge accomplishment. I was able to walk beside people without anyone holding onto me! At this point, I thought that all I would have to do would be to keep working on everything, and I would be perfectly normal in no time. I was wrong.

Jennifer

"Lesions...cervical spine...high dose...prednisone..."

My neurologist had walked into my room the next day, CD with the MRI results in hand. He talked to my mom about what they had found, and she followed along, understanding much more than I did. I turned my attention back to the TV, not really wanting to know what was wrong with me quite yet. Especially if the words the doctor used were in another language or something.

I tapped my left hand onto the remote, sighing loudly when I wasn't able to push the buttons to change the channel. I shifted my arm back to resting on one of the many stuffed animals I had received as gifts throughout my hospital stay.

My mom left for a second, following the neurologist to see the results herself. Shortly after she came back, a bunch of nurses came in to hook my IV up to a large bag filled with liquid hanging on something that resembled a coat hook with wheels. My mom peeked at the words on the bag, and exclaimed, "6500 milligrams? Isn't that a lot of Prednisone?"

So that was Prednisone. The liquid in the bag on the coat hook thing.

"We're treating her as if the inflammation in her spine was from, say, a bad car crash," the neurologist replied as he headed out of my room.

Sarah Todd

I started to gain strength in my right hand. When I was in the PICU, my knuckles had started to jump. That was when we knew movement in that hand was coming back.

By now I could almost hold a marker in my right hand. It had to be fat, though, because I didn't have enough of a grip to hold something tiny or thin.

However, even though I could walk a little, I was still in a wheelchair. It was pink! Luckily, by now I could hold my neck up. This was around the fourth week of my stay, and my second in the rehab unit.

I used my feet to move myself around in the wheelchair. At first, I was really slow, but after some practice I was so fast everyone called me "Speedy Gonzales"!

I don't know if I really wanted to be called "Speedy Gonzales", though. I would have rather been called a miracle.

"The distance is nothing; it's only the first step that is difficult."

- Marquise du Deffand

Jennifer

That night I realized just how much incredibly high doses of Prednisone can affect a person.

I fell asleep with as much ease as I had any other day in the hospital, which wasn't much, but wasn't abnormally difficult either. My mom had to help reposition my arms a couple times to keep a pain to a minimum, but that was no different.

My dreams were faded, lacking the normal sharp clarity. I woke up in the middle of the night and, still half asleep, noticed that my right hand looked very, very different.

"It's a fish! A goldfish! My right hand is a goldfish!" I exclaimed, blinking a few times. The image faded, leaving my hand looking just like it had the day before. My mom woke up, slightly confused, but fell back asleep when I didn't say anything more. In no time I was asleep again, too, dismissing the strange hallucination.

But it wasn't long before I woke up a second time. I was delusional again, but this time in a different, scarier way.

"They're trying to kill me!" I cried. My mom awoke again, and she tried to calm me down by talking to me. But it didn't work. I thought that the doctors were trying to harm me with their medicines and fancy gadgets, and I was really, really scared. And having a major freak-out attack.

My mom, unable to calm me, called some nurses in. Two walked into our room only seconds later and tried to reason with me. I guess they didn't understand that this insane, medicine-induced side of me could not be reasoned with. They told me that if I didn't calm down, they would have to sedate me.

They probably shouldn't have said anything, because the last thing I wanted was more medicine. But they did end up giving me a very minor sedative, like Bena-dryl or something, and before I knew it I was asleep again.

Sarah Todd

In the hospital there were clowns that would come to visit me sometimes throughout the day. They were dressed up as doctor clowns. Sometimes they could be pretty funny, but other times they could get so annoying!

One man who worked in the hospital wasn't ever annoying, he was hilarious! He could make elephant sounds with his mouth, and do a fake trunk with his arm! He also put coins on his forehead and they would stick! He had so many funny tricks, and they cheered me and a lot of other kids up.

Since it was a children's hospital, the hospital I stayed at had many things for kids to do. It had an outdoor fountain, an outdoor pond with a mini golf area, and a place called "The Zone" where they held contests and people could bake or do arts and crafts.

There was also a chapel where services were held on Sundays. Once for therapy on a Sunday I played piano there. I did not like it at all because I had to sit up to play, and that was a very difficult task at the time. I also didn't really play the piano, I just had to sit on the piano bench with the music therapist. I often cried while sitting up because my neck hurt so bad! What made me feel even more sad was that before I got sick I used to play the piano. I had just gotten really good at it, too, and I had my piano recital two days before I got sick.

Anyway, I remember doing prayers during the services. We did prayers for all the children to get better. I remember looking around while feeling miserable at the piano, and seeing parents crying. All I could think was that their child had passed away, or was in terrible condition. The church services were very sad. I just hoped the prayers would help.

Jennifer

The clock read 7:00 when the nurses came storming into my room to take my vitals, just as they had every morning during my hospital stay. The first nurse drew a couple vials of blood. The next nurse took my temperature and blood pressure. The next checked my reflexes. Finally they were done, but despite how tired I'd been from waking up so early I couldn't fall back asleep.

Another doctor came in, only a little while after the nurses had left. My mom muted the TV, which she'd turned on after the nurses had left.

"Hello, Jennifer!" The doctor said to me, smiling. I said hi back, and he started evaluating me.

"Okay, can you wiggle your toes? Good. Now, can you push your foot up against my hand? Great! Now kick my hand with your leg. Good again."

When we finished the leg stuff, he moved onto my arms.

"Can you squeeze my fingers with your left hand? Okay, that's good. Now your right. Squeeze as hard as you can."

My right fingers hung limply on his hand. I couldn't move them at all, let alone squeeze my fingers together. He nodded, then tested my strength in my shoulders, elbows, and wrists. When he finished with that he asked me to sit up.

My core felt numb, and felt tingly and tight when I squeezed it to attempt sitting up. Slowly I felt myself rise without any help from others, something that had been incredibly hard before. Finally, I was up, smiling like crazy. The doctor smiled too, then asked me if I could walk.

He helped me climb out of the hospital bed and held onto me as I stood up. He let go, and my legs collapsed. Oh, well. Soon.

Sarah Todd

It was about my fifth week in the rehab unit when I started to have weird swallowing problems. I would get scared whenever I swallowed food because I thought I was choking!

I also had anxiety attacks, which meant that I would freak out every five seconds or so because I was scared, and I felt like I couldn't breathe. The attacks made me have trouble sleeping.

I had been in the hospital way too long. I just couldn't take it anymore! I'd had so many painful and unpleasant tests like blood draws, MRI's, and IV's. I needed to get home. FAST!

"We are all motivated by a keen desire for praise, and the better a man is, the more he
is inspired to glory"

-Cicero

Jennifer

First it was called "ADEM", which stands for "Acute Disseminated Enceph-
alomyelitis". Later, though, they realized that my lesions didn't match those of people
with ADEM, because I had none in the brain. I only had them in my spine. So, they
switched my diagnosis to Transverse Myelitis. I was pretty glad about that, because
the new diagnosis was easier to say and spell!

I just hoped that, knowing the diagnosis now, I would be able to recover and
get out of the hospital very, very soon.

"The greatest of faults, I should say, is to be conscious of none"

-Thomas Carlyle

Sarah Todd

During my hospital stay in the rehab unit, I had many pains in my right hand and fingers. It felt like strings were coming out of my fingertips! I couldn't see them, but it just felt like there were strings. My mom kept holding up my hand and showing me that there weren't any strings, but I was scared and couldn't stop thinking about it. So, I just couldn't get across to my mom and dad that I knew that they weren't real. They did feel pretty real, though. Sometimes it would feel like the strings were tangled up around my fingers.

I also was very sensitive to pain after I regained some sensation. Once I had a tiny finger prick done for a test, and my finger hurt for days! It hurt so bad that I would cry and couldn't think about anything else. We later on learned that these funny pains and sensations were called nerve pains. Just funny little pains that you receive while your nerves are regaining feeling. That was yet another side effect of Transverse Myelitis.

"If you would create something,
you must be something"
-Johann Wolfgang von Goethe

Jennifer

IVs stink. In general they just stink. Actually, anything involving a needle stinks.

I had an IV all through my hospital stay to feed me my Prednisone which, may I remind you, was not my absolute favorite drug. The side effects were so scary but I knew that it helped me recover greatly, so the fear had to be beside the point.

When I first got my IV in, the doctors put it in my left arm. My left side of my body seemed to be slightly stronger but was completely numb to pain and temperature. I couldn't feel either! So it was ideal for shots, finger pricks, and, of course, IVs. The only downside with having my left arm hooked up to a tube whenever it was time for my Prednisone dose was that it was my stronger arm, so I couldn't do much during those times. Luckily, they didn't last too long, so I didn't really mind.

One day, though, I did. A therapy dog came into my hospital room, followed by a couple nurses, at the perfect time- when I was getting my Prednisone treatment. The dog was super sweet, and she really brightened my mood! She lied down beside me on my hospital bed, and her fur was so soft looking that I really badly wanted to pet her. But I couldn't. My left arm was hooked up to the IV pole and my right arm was completely paralyzed. Feeling bad, one nurse gently lifted my right arm up and ran my hand against the sweet dog's fur, but it wasn't the same. Still, I tried to enjoy myself, and the therapy dog's visit was much too short.

That night, thinking it would be helpful, the doctors and my mom decided to take the IV out of my left arm and put one in my right arm so I could do as much as possible when hooked up. Knowing my right arm was over-sensitive, I panicked, but they stuck it in anyway. For the rest of the night I was in immense pain, and tried to talk to my dad on the phone while ice packs were layered on my throbbing arm while it passed, but distracting myself could only help so much.

> "The man is happiest who lives from day to day and asks no more, garnering the simple goodness of life"
>
> -Euripides

Sarah Todd

Many hours a day of therapy. Ongoing tests. Hardly any rest.

The only thing that made me happy was the visitors. Well, besides the ICEEs they had in the cafeteria, because I loved those, but visitors were way better!

My room was piled with balloons, gifts, and food. Everyone loved and cared about me so much! I had a visitor almost every day. Usually, it was my grandma and grandpa, brothers, dad, my friends, my mom's friends, or a priest from my brother's school. I had never even met him before he came to see me, but he gave me a stuffed dog named by him: Prayer Buddy. Such a special man, and a special gift.

Jennifer

As if my MRI experience wasn't bad enough, not to mention my experiences with the Prednisone they had to give me, I now had to have a spinal tap. I had no idea what that was, and really didn't want to. I later learned that it was painful and extremely uncomfortable. But I was used to that by now, right?

Anyway, a bunch of my friends were visiting, as well as my grandma Kate, when I was called in for the spinal tap. A nurse came into my room, and my mom helped me get into a wheelchair to wheel me over to the room. The room was much, much smaller than I had expected.

When we got there, nurses asked me if I wanted to sit or lie on the small, three-foot long metal table that was inside the room. I opted for sitting, which I was proud of being able to do myself for short amounts of time now, because with the size of the table, my legs would have been hanging off of it!

By now, my mom had left. I had been scared for her to leave me, which was an appropriate emotion for what was about to happen.

> "Just close your eyes and enjoy the roller coaster that is life"
> - Zayn Malik

Sarah Todd

There was one type of therapy that was really fun! Music therapy! I love to sing, and at the time I really loved Taylor Swift. So, I would always sing "You Belong With Me" while the music therapist played the guitar. I memorized the whole song, and sang it for my parents. They thought that I was pretty good! It was something I could do to take my mind off of everything that was going on.

Singing is one of those things that cheers me up no matter what's happening. At times now, I'll still sing to get my mind off of things. I really love One Direction, and I always sing their songs. It's my dream to meet them someday.

Jennifer

My mom was gone. Back to our room, I assumed. A nurse put something in my IV, something that was supposed to be calming. I didn't feel any different, though. Or maybe I did. But it definitely wasn't calming. If anything, I felt more alert than before! More alert, and maybe just a teeny bit crazy.

They told me to lean forward. I did, but I had ants in my pants the whole time. They started the spinal tap, and I have to tell you, that was the worst pain ever! Seriously, it hurt so bad, I felt like screaming, and I was so alert I could tell you every detail of it. I remember those couple minutes of sheer agony better than I can remember what I had for lunch yesterday, which goes to show how the "calming" medicine worked.

Finally, it was over. My mom came to get me, and she wheeled me back to the room. My friends left while she was wheeling me back in, because I was crying. Or trying not to, anyway.

I had to lie flat on my back in bed all night after that, mostly because I now had, like, a hole in my back. I watched a movie with my mom and grandma, who had stayed, and slowly drifted to sleep.

Sarah Todd

The next morning was the day that a few kids from the rehab unit got to go on an outing, and I was one of them. We were going to spend the day at Fern Bank, a dinosaur museum. I had already been there before, but it had been a while, and I figured anything was better than staying at that stinking hospital! However, I did wish we were going somewhere different.

Anyway, that morning we all loaded on the bus, and I had to sit in a large booster seat because of my height. I had already grown out of them, so I was upset! I was also very scared about being on the bus because I hadn't been on the road in a long time! At one point I felt like I couldn't breathe! I ended up sitting on my mom's lap. Sadly, my dad had stayed home.

When we finally arrived we ate, watched an IMAX movie, and looked around the gift shop. Finally, it was time to leave. I ended up really liking leaving the hospital, but didn't enjoy the outing very much!

After the long ride back, I sat with some of the nurses and talked. During the hospital stay, I had found that I really enjoyed sitting with the nurses at their desks. It was fun! We would do mad-libs or just chat.

That day I was sitting with the nurses and I told them how long I had been at the hospital. One nurse found something that made me the happiest little girl in a wheelchair ever! I couldn't wait to tell my parents what they had been wanting to know ever since I had gone into the hospital!

Jennifer

How many kids in that hospital of mine couldn't use their hands?

None, apparently. How did I know this?

"Hi, sweetie! I'm nurse Martha. I got a calendar you can color in and some markers to draw in it!"

"Hello! I'm nurse Susan. I got you some cards to play with!"

"Hi! I'm nurse Barbara. You must be really bored being cooped up in this hospital room for so long. I brought you some paint and little paint brushes and a pad of paper to spend the time!"

"Hello! I'm Kimmy. I'm a magician! Want to see some tricks? Pick a card. Just grab it. Take one. Oh, you can't? Okay, I'll pick it for you. Wasn't that cool? Here's your own magic trick to work on!"

It seemed like every form of entertainment they tried to bring me involved using my hands! I guess I could have used my feet for some things, but trying to hold a little paintbrush in between my toes would probably frustrate me. And I was already frustrated enough as it was!

However, even if I could color in a coloring book calendar thing, I probably wouldn't have wanted to. All I was looking forward to doing every day was spending time with visitors and being wheeled around my hospital floor. And therapy. I liked therapy, because my therapists, unlike my doctors, really believed in me. They believed that with enough hard work and dedication, I could walk again, and maybe get my hands back to normal, or at least almost normal. And those were all just steps forward to running again.

"Without inspiration the best powers of the mind remain dormant. There is a fuel in us which needs to be ignited by sparks"

-Johann Gottfried Von Herder

Sarah Todd

I wheeled down the hallway to my room where my parents stood. I excitedly informed them of what the nurse had said to me earlier.

"Mommy, Daddy, I'm going home on June ninth!"

They were so happy and, of course, so was I.

"One more week," I repeated over and over in my head. "One more week."

"I can do this," I said to myself. "I've already done six!"

It just seemed so long.

"I can do it. I can do it. I know I can. I believe I can," Over and over and over in my mind.

Jennifer

I hated, hated, hated being cooped up in that hospital room with the plain white walls, small windows, and classic hospital smell. I asked my mom to wheel me around my floor all the time, just to get out. One day, one of the nurses had a better idea.

"There's a balcony that you can get to from this floor. Might be nice to get some fresh air."

That didn't seem like a bad idea at all to me, so my mom wheeled me out to the balcony. It was fairly large, with different games like hopscotch and bag-o lining the floor. A couple tables surrounded by chairs sat near the four-foot tall wall surrounding the balcony.

When we arrived outside the fresh air hit me, something I hadn't even known I'd missed. I breathed it in, then stuck my legs off the edge of the wheelchair and moved them across the ground to propel the chair forward. I wheeled myself that way towards the edge of the balcony. Feet still flat on the ground, I pushed myself up out of the wheelchair. I leaned on the ledge, resting my arms on top of it. I was standing. The warm August breeze whipped my hair around slightly and I smiled, not wanting the moment to end.

"Go back a little to leap further"

-John Clarke

Sarah Todd

Finally, it was the night of June eighth. I got tucked into the uncomfortable hospital bed for the last time. I kept laughing and smiling and thinking, "I'm going home tomorrow!"

It took me forever to fall asleep. I was just so excited! I finally fell asleep at around midnight, two hours after I had been tucked in bed! I kept waking up throughout the night, too, once at two in the morning, then four, then six, then, finally, seven o'clock. It was a horrible night's sleep. I was just so excited!

When I woke up for good, my mom was up getting dressed. I said 'good morning' to her, eager to get out of bed so I could say my goodbyes to everyone in the hospital. It took nearly two hours! I was so happy to go home, but also sad to leave those wonderful people who had cared and helped me for those long fifty days.

My dad and John came into the room to help clear it of balloons, gifts, and leftover food, amongst other things. We set it all in a wagon, collected the papers from the doctor, and were off to the elevator! We took my wheelchair and walker home, just in case, but I no longer needed them. I walked right out of that hospital all because of the best PT ever!

Jennifer

The biggest thing that comes with Transverse Myelitis, or at least the thing most obvious to outsiders, is paralysis. However, there are many other symptoms, too. Fatigue is a big one, and so are the effects of the nerves going haywire. These effects range from all sorts of pains to just random, odd sensations.

For some reason I couldn't detect temperature in my scalp during those early days in the hospital. My mom figured it out when she washed my hair with warm water one day and I complained of it being ice-cold. Not being able to have my hair comfortably washed was annoying for both of us, although I insisted for a long time that she kept using cold water. This was just one of many annoyances and difficulties with my nerves... And Transverse Myelitis in general.

Even so, I knew that it was going to get better, because by now most of my problems were! Very shortly after having been put on the Prednisone I noticed a lot of good changes. Very soon I could walk. Not long distances, but at least from the bed to the bathroom with minimal help from my mom.

Within a couple days, my left hand got significantly better. I could feed my-self without as much of a mess, I could kind of hold a couple cards, could dress my-self (in about five times the amount of time as a normal person, but still), and, to-wards the end of my stay, had enough finger strength to finally push the buttons on the TV remote! My nerves may have been annoying me greatly, but my list of suc-cesses was growing by the minute, and that made me very, very happy.

Sarah Todd

My mom was crying tears of joy. My dad pulled the car up, and my mom helped me in. I was very eager to get those hospital bracelets off, but had to wait until I got home, where there were scissors.

I was finally riding down the highway to home. I was happy to get home, but also scared to be riding in a car again after not for fifty days! I started to get another anxiety attack, much like the ones in the hospital. To keep me comfortable, John and I played the "Alphabet Game" on the way home. To play this game, you need to find a license plate or sign first with the letter 'A', then 'B', and so on. Whoever reaches 'Z' first wins! We didn't get to finish the game before we got home, though.

We entered our neighborhood and drove through it to our house. Because we live pretty deep into it, it took almost two minutes to get home after we reached the neighborhood.

As we drove into the driveway, I saw a surprise waiting for me. A big surprise!

Jennifer

I had visitors almost every day in the hospital, and they always heightened my mood. Some days, I had more than one. Once I had six.

That day started with my aunt Liz and her best friend Loren coming. Liz came with a couple athletic headbands and a new purple running t-shirt, as well as a bag filled with balloons. Each balloon was filled with something different: one had flour, one had brown sugar, one had hair gel, etc. I squeezed each one and tried to guess what they were filled with. It was actually a pretty fun game, and it gave me something to do for some time.

When I was finished with that, Cathy and her kids Andy and Sophia, who had been some of our family's closest friends since birth, came over. I asked my mom if I could take them all out to the balcony, and she said yes, so I made my way to the bathroom to get changed to go outside.

It took a while, but I got myself changed into new shorts and a loose t-shirt. When I got out of the bathroom, what I saw in my bed made me laugh really hard. My aunt had stuffed a couple stuffed animals into the new purple T-shirt, leaving the head of one sticking out the head hole of the shirt. She had lined a couple pillows under the blanket, which had been pulled up to the edge of the stuffed shirt. It looked like somebody with a hedgehog head was lying in my bed.

We decided to leave that in my bed while we walked over to the balcony. We brought a pack of cards with us, and when we got outside we sat down at one of the tables to play them. Halfway through a game of "Spoons", which we decided every-one had to sit on one of their hands so they would have to play it the same way as me, my godmother Nicolle came outside.

She was laughing, and told us that when she came up to the room to find us a nurse had told her that I was sleeping. The set-up my aunt Liz had constructed with stuffed animals and pillows had tricked her! I laughed the whole way back to my hospital room.

Sarah Todd

There was a huge sign on the garage door that read, "Welcome Home, Sarah Todd!" with about fifty handprints and names surrounding the message. There were balloons, candy, notes, and chalk drawings on the driveway there! One of the notes read, "On cloud nine that you will get home soon!"

I was so happy, and pleasantly surprised! My mom was crying tears of joy while my grandma Katie hugged her.

"I'm just so happy we're home!" my mom said, tearing up.

I went inside and into every room in the house! I saw that my brothers were outside and my dog, Buddy, was inside. He's a Havaneese, and was about eleven months old at the time.

After I explored my house, I wanted to go across the street to my friend Alex's house. However, my mom said to me, "Hold on! We just got home! You can't just go roaming around by yourself yet!"

Instead, we all went inside to chat. We talked about how wonderful everything was. We found out that our neighbor had set the whole thing up. She also set up meals to be donated to us, which had started when I was in the hospital and my grandparents had taken care of my brothers.

I just loved being home! It had the most comfortable bed and the best food ever!

"We will go to the moon and do other things, not because they are easy but because they are hard."

- John F. Kennedy, Jr.

Jennifer

Of course, I had therapy at the hospital. The first therapist I saw was an occupational therapist. She gave me a large splint to wear on my right hand at night.

The second I saw was a physical therapist. She put a "gait belt" on me and held onto it to help me walk better without worrying about falling. In no time at all I lost the belt and could walk around my floor with the only trouble being an annoying numbness around my trunk, like somebody put plastic wrap around me and squeezed!

The third I saw was another OT. He stretched my super tight right shoulder and wrist, gave me little exercises to further help my arms, and put Kinesio Tape on my right shoulder to push it down. The first taping I didn't like as much, but the second really relaxed my shoulder. I wore that one until I went home. Home, the best place on earth, and the place with the most comfortable bed ever!

Sarah Todd

The night of June ninth, 2010, my mom slept in my room with me.

I had a lot of trouble sleeping the next couple weeks. My mom sat in a rocking chair in my room, because I was so used to her sleeping with me when I was in the hospital.

I needed help going up the stairs, and I needed to wear my tennis shoes and gait belt every second of the day. Since I had to keep those things on, dancing could not happen yet.

My mom also put "resting chairs" in the hallway, but I didn't really need them. They were just a precaution.

The day after I got home, I had to go to a rehab facility to do therapy from nine in the morning to one in the afternoon. It was extremely boring the first day because I was just evaluated, and I hadn't made any friends yet. I thought that all of this would be over soon, but it was just the beginning for my family and I.

Jennifer

I don't know how likely it is to ever surprise a neurologist. They see tons of patients every day, and see a lot of the same things, too.

My neurologist originally told us not to get our hopes up. He said that there was a chance I might not be able to walk again, my left hand probably would never get as strong or have as much dexterity as we were hoping, and my right would always be a flop. Nothing. Not even a twitch in the shoulder, which was how it was at first.

When my mom went with him to go over test results, she told him I was getting way better. He told her that that was not very likely.

He came in to see me, though, and was very pleasantly surprised! He even said it took a lot to impress him, and we passed that test!

When it was time to go home, I was so much better than I was on August sixteenth. My left hand and arm, if you didn't look too closely, seemed to have almost perfect movement, and probably almost half the strength that it used to have.

By now my legs were almost perfect! I could walk around my whole floor of the hospital a couple times without getting too tired now, and didn't fall down when I walked.

My trunk was still pretty weak. I could sit up for long periods of time by now, luckily, but it still had some numbness. I also still had a little bit of a squeezing sensation, like somebody wrapped my core with plastic wrap and pulled.

My right hand and shoulder still had no movement at all. I could, however, move my elbow a little bit. That gave me a lot of hope.

Pretty much the whole left side of my body was still numb to pain and temperature. I couldn't feel heat or cold on that side, which felt really odd in the shower; I also couldn't feel when I was poked with needles and stuff. I could, contrary to what almost everyone seemed to think when my pain/temperature problem was mentioned, feel it when people touched me. It wasn't numb, exactly. I just couldn't feel the extremes.

Another thing I was left with was extreme nerve pains. Nothing helped them, and they were so random and all over the place that it would be hard to do anything anyway. At this point, though, they weren't nearly as bad as they would become later on, once scar-tissue had formed. That was the one thing that got worse after August 16th, 2011.

When I was released from the hospital, my grandma took me home. My mom had left a couple hours earlier to get her car from the other hospital.

We packed up our things, got the IV I'd had on my arm from the moment I got to the hospital out, got papers and whatever, and left. As we approached the garage my grandma had left her car, she asked if I wanted to be wheeled out in a wheelchair. I told her that I wanted to walk out.

In the end, we got the wheelchair. I didn't sit in it, though. We used it to hold the million things we had to bring to the car.

However, walking out of the hospital would show me that my body was still not quite as strong as I'd thought it was. There were still going to be challenges. There were going to be challenges for a long time.

Sarah Todd

After I got out of the hospital, my grandma Katie and I were talking. She told me that since my mom was so busy while I was in the hospital, she had to run some errands for her. One of those errands was returning something to Target. However, the item she needed to return was past the 90-day return deadline. So, my grandma explained to the worker that I, her granddaughter, was in the hospital so my mom didn't have any time to return the item. She said that I had a spinal cord injury and that I all of a sudden couldn't move one day. After letting my grandma return the item, the worker asked, "Is it Transverse Myelitis?"

My grandma said, "Yes, I thought nobody had heard of it!"

"My husband has it," the employee replied.

After my grandma told me that story, I couldn't believe that somebody other than my family had heard of Transverse Myelitis.

Jennifer

After what felt to me like a long time of searching and walking, we found my grandma's car in the huge parking garage.

My grandma unlocked and opened the doors, and I sunk into the soft seats. We left the garage, left the hospital, and then left the town. Everything that had happened in the last week was behind me. Well, besides the obvious.

After sitting in the car for a while, my tailbone started to hurt really bad. I shoved a rolled up sweater underneath me to try to keep the pain down. Luckily, the drive wasn't too much longer.

When I entered the door to my house, my whole family greeted me with a sign behind them that said, "Welcome home, Jen!" along with some cute pictures my little siblings drew.

I greeted my whole family. I had missed them so much! My brother, Reese, who was twelve years old at the time; my brother, Harrison, who was nine; my brother, Tristan, who was six; my brother, Bryce, who was four; my sister, Jolie, who was two; and my daddy had all taken the time to make the signs and greet me at the door.

Now I was home, and I thought my adventure was over, at least for the most part. Little did I know it was just the opposite and had, in fact, just begun.

Part
2
Life with TM

"Hope is like the sun, which, as we journey through it, casts the shadow of our burden behind us"

-Samuel Smiles

Sarah Todd

I woke up crying the next morning because I didn't want to go to day rehab. We had to wake up at seven thirty and leave at eight in order to get there on time. The place was only twenty-five minutes away, but there was a lot of traffic on the highway in the morning.

My parents walked into the rehab facility with me, then left me. They would come back at one-thirty. I was scared to be there without them.

We all got a schedule in the morning that told us who we were going to see that day, when we were going to see them, and where. Sometimes, we had therapy in groups, but I didn't like that very much.

When it was lunch time we went to the eating area, where we ordered food. I was mad, because most of us had just gotten home from the hospital, and we had to continue to eat slop! I wished I could pack a lunch.

I still hadn't made any friends, but I recognized a few kids from the hospital.

Therapy was extremely boring. The therapists tried to make it fun and play games, but it didn't work. "How long will I have to be at this place?" I thought to myself. The answer was quite awhile.

Jennifer

As much as I hated to admit it, I still definitely needed therapy. I had received some in the hospital, but not nearly as much as I needed.

When we got home, we ended up doing PT two times a week (Wednesdays and Fridays) and OT two times a week (Mondays and Thursdays). We went to Athletico for each, but in different locations because the one I went to for physical therapy did not have occupational therapy.

Right before I got sick, my dad had knee surgery. So, of course, he had to have therapy, too. He went to Athletico for PT, and one day I went with him to check it out. This was only a couple days before I was going to go there myself, and I wanted to meet the people there and see how everything worked. I really liked the place, and the people there were incredibly nice, too! This proved to be a good thing, because I was going to be going there for quite a while.

Sarah Todd

Right after Father's Day, I had a huge "Welcome Home" party! My mom invited a bunch of neighbors, friends, and family. Most of the time, I played the Wii with the girls that had come, while the boys stayed in the kitchen with everyone else. At this point I could just barely get my right arm up to put food in my mouth. My arm got tired easily, but at least I could feed myself!

The guests all brought a ton of cards, food, and gifts. I sure had my share of those things! It also felt so good to see everyone again! I'm sure my mom agreed, too, because she spent the whole time talking to everyone! On the other hand, Alex and John barely said a word, mostly because they didn't really know anybody.

At this party, I was surprised to find that I was shy around my own friends! I hadn't seen them in so long! I felt kind of sad.

I ended up really liking this "Welcome Home" party! It was a huge gift on it's own! Even though I had known about it, I still found it very amazing. It had been hard to find a good date for it because it was right after Father's Day, and I was really glad it had worked out. It was just so awesome, and couldn't have been better.

Jennifer

The day after I first went to the hospital I was supposed to have "surgery" for an ingrown toenail. Of course, I really couldn't do that, so because the toenail didn't miraculously heal during my hospital stay (it felt a million times better than a couple days before I got sick though, probably because I had much worse things to worry about), it had to be rescheduled.

A little less than a week after I got home from the hospital my grandma took me to the rescheduled appointment. When we arrived we filled out some paperwork and waited in the waiting room until they called me in to start. When we got to the room we waited even longer until a doctor finally came in to talk to us.

He examined my toe, then left for a second, and came back with a nurse carrying a shot with the biggest needle I had seen in my life. I seriously felt like it was two feet tall, although I may be exaggerating just a tiny bit.

He said it was a numbing shot, and that it might feel like a little bee sting when he first stuck it in my toe, but that would be the only pain I would feel because it would make it so that I would not be able to feel my whole right foot.

When he poked me, I almost screamed. The doctor looked surprised; it wasn't supposed to hurt that much. But to me, it did. Of course the messed up toenail had to be on the more sensitive side of my body. The nurse came back in and gave me a lollipop to bite on and a magazine to distract me. Neither really helped. The doctor came back in and asked me if my toe felt numb. I said no. It didn't. Not fully believing me, he asked me to close my eyes and tell him if I felt anything as he brushed his finger against my toe. I felt it, and told him, so he gave me another numbing shot. Luckily this didn't hurt quite as bad as the other one, because it was already partially numb.

After the numbing was in place, he started the procedure. It was strange. I wasn't supposed to feel anything at all. And it was true that I couldn't feel my right foot at all. However, my opposite toe, the big one on my left foot, kept stinging. I didn't say anything yet, but it was then that I realized that my messed-up nerves might end up being a bigger problem than I had thought.

"When one door of happiness closes, another opens, but often we look so long at the closed door that we do not see the one that has been opened for us"

-Helen Keller

Sarah Todd

Weeks passed by, and I was still going to day-rehab. Still, there was yucky hospital food, therapy, and no real friends for me. I hated it. Luckily, by now it was July thirtieth, and I was going to graduate from day rehab the next day! This means that I was well enough to go on to outpatient therapy to do hour-long therapy sessions. I would do this around four times a week. I would now have to drive thirty minutes there, spend an hour doing therapy, and drive thirty minutes back. There would be a lot of driving around, so much that I could have two therapy sessions in the amount of time I would spend in the car! Still, I would now be gone from home two hours a couple times a week instead of the six I was used to at the rehab facility. I couldn't wait to graduate from day-rehab and move on to different people, different scenery, and new therapy methods.

Finally, it was the day of July thirty-first, 2010, and the day I was going to graduate!

As always, I woke up at seven-thirty. My mom helped me get dressed, brush my teeth, and get my socks and shoes on in order to hop in the car at eight o'clock. Like always, I did therapy that day, but I was able to tell everyone that it was my graduation day!

At one-thirty, my parents arrived to watch me graduate. The rehab nurse helped me dress in a purple cap and gown. Everyone gathered around in the main gym. I sat in a chair in front of everyone and listened to the therapists talk about how great I did and all the things I accomplished at day-rehab.

"When I saw you go up on your tiptoes like you do in ballet, I was amazed!" my PT, Cindy, said.

The therapists there were my PT's, Cindy and Michelle, and my OT's, Rebecca and Bahvika. PT, physical therapy, worked mostly my legs, feet, back, trunk, and chest; OT, occupational therapy, worked my hands, arms, and shoulders. At rehab, I liked PT better because it was easier for me.

After all the therapists said great things about me, the nurse gave me a big kiss, leaving lipstick on my cheek.

The graduation was now over, and it was time to say my goodbyes. Afterward, I thought about what Cindy had said, and how happy I was about her compliment. It was just that day that I was able to get up on my tiptoes. That meant one thing to me. I would be able to dance again!

"Lord! We know what we are, but know not what we may be"

-William Shakespeare

Jennifer

The day after I got home from the hospital was the first day of school. I begged my mom to let me go, because it would be my last first day at the K-8 school I'd been at for so long!

But 8th grade would have to wait, because the school wouldn't even let me in until they had a meeting with my mom and all that. In the end, it was decided that I would go to school a couple days after it started, and then ease in to the day by starting with only going to two periods, and going up from there, and most likely going only for half of each day for a long time.

Everyone at the school was really nice, as everyone at that awesome school always was. I just couldn't wait to go to school all day, every day, so my life would have a sense of normalcy again.

Finally, it was my first day of school. For most kids, it was the third day of school, but for me, it was the first.

I was extremely nervous, of course. I went in early with my mom, where the principal helped me open my locker and get comfortable seats for first period. First period was science class, and we had class in the lab where the only seats were high, backless stools. It made sense for me to have a different chair.

I also met my homeroom teacher, who was the only teacher I didn't already know. I'd had all of my other teachers the year before, because seventh grade and eighth grade were combined, at least for the most part.

The second bell rang, signaling that everyone start going to their classes. I stood nervously next to my chair, wondering if anyone would see me and ask why I was in the classroom early, or why I hadn't been at school the first few days.

Nobody did, though. Kids started filing into their homerooms, sitting at desks and talking to their friends. I sat down, a little more at ease, but not much. All of these kids were the same as they were the year before. How could everyone else's lives still be the same, when I had just had a life-changing experience?

"No longer forward nor behind
I look in hope and fear;
But grateful take the good I find,
The best of now and here."
-John G. Whittier

Sarah Todd

I was very excited when I got home from day-rehab. I didn't dance that day, but I got really into playing "Just Dance" on my Wii. My mom would help me do the parts using arms when we played, while I did the leg parts. One of the songs in the game was "Cotten-eyed Joe", and that was my favorite one to dance to. I had to do a lot of stomping in that song, so it was the easiest one in the game, since my legs were better than my arms. I played "Just Dance" a lot.

A few days after being released from day-rehab, my dad and I were sitting in the family room doing pretty much nothing. I decided to ask him if I could try to dance for a little while.

"Well, I guess so," was his reply. "Be careful!" He stayed in the room.

My dad turned the TV on for me and set up my *Cinderella* DVD. I picked the "Summer Dance", which was less than a minute long. When I finished dancing to that song, I asked my dad to leave. I preferred not to have an audience.

So, my dad went to sit on the porch with my mom. He probably told her that I was attempting to dance again, and I'm sure they were both scared that I would fall.

I did a left arabesque and jumped up while doing it. I realized that it was a little bit more difficult than on my right side.

I still remembered every single dance in all of my shows, even though I hadn't danced in nearly four months! I got tired quickly, so I took a break and sat on the couch. I was really happy that I could finally dance again, but I knew I would have to do a lot of work to catch up to where I was before I got Transverse Myelitis.

"A wise man will make more opportunities than he finds"

-Francis Bacon

Jennifer

Many things that were so easy before, things that I didn't even notice, were now a challenge. I could no longer hold my textbooks, open containers, or spread peanut butter on bread without help. My two-year-old sister had to help me do things such as opening band-aids!

Paralysis wasn't my only problem, though. Another big one was the left side of my body being numb to pain and temperature. The pain one was a good thing when I had to have shots and blood draws, and I had an insane amount of blood draws, because I couldn't feel the needle. But the temperature one was awful! Showers never felt just right, because the two halves of my body felt the water temperature differently. Walking outside never felt just right, because the air temperature wasn't the same. Once I grabbed a hot bowl with my left hand and didn't realize I was almost burning myself until my left fingers tingled and, curious, I brushed my right hand onto the side of the bowl. It was really frustrating.

I kept telling myself that everything would be okay, and I would be exactly the way I had been before within three months. In the back of my mind, though, I knew that wasn't true.

"Present fears are less than horrible imaginings"

-William Shakespeare

Sarah Todd

It was time for me to go to hour-long therapy sessions. The rehab center was right next to the hospital I had been in and had multiple gyms, a large waiting room, and a lot of therapists. My mom had scheduled a few sessions with an OT and a PT.

My mom already knew quite a bit about the place because my brother, John, had been there when he was little and had Torticollis. He had had therapy there because of it.

Anyway, my mom had heard that the OT was certified for E-Stim, which is why she wanted me to have appointments with her. E-Stim is where pads are placed on the muscles that need strengthening, then are connected to wires that connect to a machine that shocks the muscles. The E-Stim isn't supposed to hurt, although it might if the machine was turned up really high!

Dana and Erin, my therapists from the hospital, had done E-Stim a few times, so I already knew about it. My nerves had been really sensitive at the time, so I really did not like E-Stim! Luckily, the OT did not do it that much. On the other hand, the PT did it a lot! I really hoped that my therapists would try to make therapy fun.

Jennifer

"Dad, are you coming to pick me up now?" I asked through my cell phone after school one day.

"Sorry Jen, you're going to have to wait until Reese comes home so he can watch the little kids, or until Ainsleigh wakes up from her nap so I can load her and the other little ones in the car," he explained. I sighed, wishing my little cousin would wake up right at that moment. Or that my brothers would sprint home instead of walk. But neither were very likely to happen.

I said bye to my dad and hung up, then leaned back on the bench outside my school to wait for him to arrive. I could tell that I was going to be there awhile.

A group of kids passed by. Runners. Cross Country runners, to be exact. They were at practice.

I stared at them longingly. The air was warm; not too hot or cold. Perfect running weather. I wanted to be out there with them really, really badly. They passed by a couple more times, looking more and more tired with each lap around the school. That was the best part of running-- getting tired. Feeling the subtle burning in your lungs and wanting to lie on a bed of ice when you stop. Those were definitely not most people's idea of fun and comfort, but I loved it. It felt familiar to me. When I stopped, as I chugged down a gallon of water, I felt proud. Proud that I had just run three miles without stopping. Proud of the tiny aches and pains that made me feel stronger. Proud of the layer of sweat covering my body; that was better than the biggest medal. Now I felt proud when I put a pair of socks on my own feet.

I looked the other direction and tried not to think about running until my dad finally came to pick me up.

"Nothing can stop the man with the right mental attitude from achieving his goal; nothing on Earth can help the man with the wrong mental attitude"

-Thomas Jefferson

Sarah Todd

My mom and dad drove me to the rehab center for my first day of therapy. There, they had a room with a bunch of mini TV's so the patients' parents could see what their kids and their therapists were doing. They would have to wear headphones to hear and type a number to the camera they wanted to view from the room. My parents came to my first appointment with my OT and watched me.

I walked with my therapist into a big gym, where we sat on a large mat. Then she began to evaluate me. First, she measured the range of motion in my arms, which is how far they can go before being tight. Then she tested how strong I was by giving me resistance with her hand and having me push really hard on it. She then rated my strength on a scale of one to five, five being the strongest. I thought I did pretty well.

Finally, she was finished with me. My PT was waiting for me right by the door.

"Hi, Sarah Todd!" she said.

"Hi!" I said back.

"I'm going to be your PT," she said.

"Nice to meet you," I said politely.

"You, too!" she responded as she began to test the range of motion in my legs. They were a teeny bit tight, but pretty good, overall. She then did the resistance test in my legs, and that seemed good, too.

I would continue going to the rehab center until April 1st, 2011.

"Struggling and suffering are an essence of a life worth living"

- Dean Karnazes

Jennifer

This day was going to be a big step for me. It was going to be the day I walked home from school with my brothers. It was a little less than a mile, which seemed long and short at the same time.

My parents didn't exactly know that I was walking home yet. I decided it on my own, in an attempt to escape the awkwardness of waiting for ages for my dad to pick me up.

I gathered up my stuff from my locker and put them in my backpack, as I had done every day since school started. I lifted my backpack up and carefully rested it on my left shoulder, knowing it could more easily take the weight than my right. I then walked downstairs and met my brothers in the multipurpose room.

My then twelve-year-old brother Reese, who was the second oldest next to me, offered to take my backpack for me after I grabbed the sling I had been given at the hospital out of the front pocket. The doctors didn't want me using it very often because it was better for my arms to hang normally, so I usually didn't. But I knew that the walk home would be much easier without my right arm hurting (it hurt a lot when it dangled normally), so I slipped it into the sling and followed my brothers out the doors of the school.

The walk was much easier than I had thought it would be. I enjoyed the fresh air, dropping a little behind my brothers. I didn't care if I was slow. Slow was better than getting fatigued and proving that I wasn't ready to walk less than a mile yet.

Finally, we were home. Reese dropped my backpack next to the dining room table and headed to the kitchen. I excitedly found my dad and told him that I had walked home. I think he was just as relieved as I was that I could do it.

Sitting down next to my backpack at the table I smiled. Running seemed so close. I could just feel it.

"Ask yourself this question: 'Will this matter a year from now?'"
-Richard Carlson, writing in "Don't Sweat the Small Stuff"

Sarah Todd

There are many things in this world that children have to do. One of these things is going to school. For me, that was another story.

In the condition I was in I could not attend third grade at the school building. My mom would have to discuss with my school principal if and how I could do my work for that year somewhere other than the school.

My mom ended up going to a meeting at Ocee Elementary School, the school I had gone to since I was in kindergarten. I really wanted to go to Ocee for third grade, too, but I knew that I couldn't. My mom and the Ocee principal would have to figure out some sort of plan otherwise.

Meanwhile, I kept wondering what they were going to come up with and how I was going to go to school. I was worried, because I always had a lot of friends at school, including Jordan. She was my best friend in second grade.

I really wanted to attend school with all my friends, like usual. There were more important issues being discussed, though, like how I was going to keep my education up.

Jennifer

School. Therapy. School. Therapy. Over and over and over again. I was juggling way too many things those first few days. Schoolwork. Fatigue. Paralysis. Therapy. Homework. Waking up early. It never seemed to end!

The worst day of the week was definitely Monday. There are obvious reasons to that, of course, like the fact that it comes right after the lovely weekend, and everyone is tired. But I had other reasons, too.

On Mondays, I had OT. Occupational therapy. Now, that might not sound that bad, especially since I also had OT on Thursdays, and PT on Wednesdays and Fridays. On Mondays, though, I had two sessions of OT, each at a different place and using completely different techniques.

Every Monday I would wake up bright and early to go to school. Then, I would go home and maybe have time to eat something before going to "Ms. Mary's". There, Ms. Mary would do some relaxing things, like massaging my arms in a soothing way to, apparently, activate the nerves. I really didn't mind it there.

Then, right after that, my mom and I would pick something up to eat. We would eat it in the car quickly so we could head over to the next place in time for my appointment.

This OT, the one right after relaxing Ms. Mary's, was anything but soothing. The OT would talk to my mom while stretching my shoulder so much, I was almost screaming! It probably seemed like something out of a comedy movie: Someone is practically writhing in pain while the other two people are chatting, having a grand old time! Looking back on it, it actually seems pretty funny to me.

After that, I would get home and be extremely tired. I would do as much homework as I could without drifting off, then go to bed and explain my situation to the teachers the next day. They always seemed to understand, but I knew there was only so much that they could.

Sarah Todd

A few days later, I had to go to the doctor's office for a follow-up appointment. My pediatrician, Dr. Penny, had been my doctor ever since I was born.

While I was there, Dr. Penny had me walk across the room and move my arms, legs, wrists, and hands. He also talked to my mom and I about all of my improvements and our concerns. One of those concerns was how I was going to go to school, and Dr. Penny suggested a home-bound tutor. This was mainly because of all the germs at school, the condition I was in, and because I couldn't really go to school when I was gone for two hours every day to go to therapy! My mom thought it was a good idea, so she reported the suggestion to my principal.

About a week or so after the appointment with Dr. Penny, my mom said she had news for me. She told me that I would have a home-bound tutor, just as the doctor suggested, come to our house every Monday and Wednesday for an hour and a half.

"Yay!" I exclaimed, after I heard the news. "Do you know who the tutor is going to be?"

"Yes," She replied. "It's going to be Ms. Stewart."

"Yay!" I said again, excitedly. Ms. Stewart had been my brother John's teacher when he was in third grade, so we all knew her very well. She was such a sweet lady, and I was also happy to know that she would have been my teacher if I was going to school like everyone else.

I got Ms. Stewart for third grade! I was so excited about it, and just couldn't wait to see her!

Jennifer

My favorite class in school had been English for a long time, but when I learned to play an instrument in fifth grade I found it hard to choose between that and band.

I had already been signed up for band in eighth grade, and the first couple weeks of school the band teacher I'd had since fifth grade was gone. Her new assistant band director took her place while she was on this leave but, although she was nice, she was someone I had never met before. Since there was no way I could finger the notes on my instrument that year, each day in band I sat on a chair and listened to everyone else play, patiently waiting for the other band director to come back.

The day she finally did I was excited, but waited until the end of the day to tell her my story. If she hadn't already heard about what had happened, I wanted her to know why I couldn't play.

I approached her and gave a very shortened explanation of my life since August sixteenth.

As it turned out, she already knew. She liked hearing the full, real story, though.

"I was at the grocery store one day in the summer," she explained, "when a little girl who must have been a sister of a band member asked me if I had heard what had happened to Jennifer Starzec. I told her I hadn't, and she said that you were sleeping for a long time and weren't waking up. That scared me a lot! I ended up getting the real story from an adult, though, luckily."

I nodded through all this, very surprised. How had that rumor started? Was it just the little girl mixing her facts up? How many other people thought that I had been in, like, a coma? My cheeks flushed at the thought, and I hoped that anyone who had heard that had gotten their facts straight. Because although Transverse Mye-litis really stunk, it was much better than some alternatives.

"A failure is a man who has blundered, but is not able to cash in on the experience"
-Elbert Hubbard

Sarah Todd

Ms. Stewart came to my house a few days later to drop off my school things. She walked in the front door and smiled, bringing workbooks, textbooks, a whiteboard, and an agenda. I was so glad to see her! We all talked for a little bit, and she told us about what time she would be coming over on Mondays and Wednesdays. Too soon, she had to leave.

Finally, it was time for my first day of third grade. My mom laid shorts and a new t-shirt out for me to wear. I loved the t-shirt so much! It had a picture of a big chocolate-chip cookie in the middle of the shirt that had arms, legs, eyes, and a mouth, and was wearing shoes and a pair of black glasses. Written above the cookie was the word "SMART", and written below it was the word "COOKIE". It was so adorable! I was so happy when my mom showed my outfit to me!

After I got dressed, my mom and I went downstairs to wait for the doorbell to ring. My mom and I had decided that Ms. Stewart and I would work at the kitchen table, and we laid out all my textbooks, workbooks, whiteboard, and agenda on it. A cup full of markers, pens, and pencils sat in the middle. It was all so perfect.

I paced back and forth through the kitchen, awaiting my tutor's arrival. Suddenly, the doorbell rang. I ran to the door.

Jennifer

It was one of those crazy Mondays again. I got up for school in the morning, then went through the normal classes like a robot. I got home and ate something quick before going to Ms. Mary's.

Afterward, my mom and I grabbed some food from an Asian restaurant. We had enough time to eat until we were full before driving to my other occupational therapist.

When my shoulder had been stretched so much I thought it was going to pop and I had done so many exercises I didn't want to even think about it, my mom and I drove home. On the way back, she told me something that made me suddenly full of energy and wishing there was no such thing as a speed limit!

When we got back, our house held all five of my siblings, like usual. My dad wasn't there, but that wasn't a surprise because I knew he went to work on Monday evenings.

One thing that was new in my house was the presence of my grandparents. They sat on the couch with a bag next to them, talking to my siblings and laughing.

When they saw me enter the door, they opened the bag and handed something to me. It was an iPad. My very own iPad! They also gave me a light green cover to attach to it. I held it in my hands, not really believing it even though my mom had already told me in the car, and had hinted at it since the hospital.

My grandparents stayed as we connected it to the computer and loaded the software onto it. When that was finally done, we bought a couple apps and took some pictures, then talked a little longer with my grandparents. It was too soon, but unfortunately it was time for them to leave.

"Bye, Mima! Bye, Beepa! Thanks!" I said before giving them each a hug. I kept waving "goodbye" to them as they climbed into their car and drove away from sight. I walked back into my house, where I found a good-sized bag for my iPad so I could bring it to school the next day. My parents had already gotten permission from the school to have me bring the iPad and use it to write anything too long for my left hand so I wouldn't have to leave my seat to use one of the computers that were held in each classroom. I was extremely grateful.

Sarah Todd

My mom grabbed the keys and made her way to the front door. As I followed her, she opened the door, and there was Ms. Stewart, waiting with a huge grin on her face.

"Hi!" she said as she reached out and squeezed me really tight. She seemed very happy to see me, and I was happy to see her!

We stood and chatted for a few minutes, then brought her over to the kitchen and explained our work space. Finally, Ms. Stewart and I sat down and began some math. Now, even though I was recovering from a spinal cord injury, I was a year ahead in most of my subjects, so what we were about to do that year was not traditional third-grade math.

"126 + 234 = 360..." We started, "8 * 7 = 56..."

Ugh, I thought, first day back and thinking, thinking, thinking! Summer just gave the freedom to be lazy, sleep in, and do whatever! Ah, summer. One of the best seasons! Well, other than spring, of course, but that has its own reasons.

"You know," Ms. Stewart cut in, "A good way to remember 8 * 7 is that movie, A Christmas Story! Have you seen it?"

"Yes," I replied.

"Okay, then just remember the scene where all the boys are in class and they all say, 'eight times seven is fifty-six'," she pointed out. I laughed, and later realized that she always managed to crack me up!

Anyway, I had a lot of fun with Ms. Stewart that Monday. I ended up loving her so much! She stayed for a short hour and a half, then left. By that time, it was 5:00. I would see her on Wednesday.

Jennifer

My dad was always interested in helping me get better. He did exercises with me, one of them being one where he had me simply trying to lift my right arm to a pull-up bar and try to keep it there. It sounds simple, but for someone who couldn't move her arm a millimeter on her own a month before, it wasn't.

I would stand under the bar and try to lift my arm up. After I got it as high as I could on my own, my dad would just barely guide it up there until I could hold onto the bar. I couldn't yet move any of my fingers, so I had to use my left hand to hold it there, but it was helping still the same.

My dad also had me try to pick a stuffed animal up with my right hand. It was hard, and I was only able to pick it up by latching my hand onto it like a claw, but I could still do it, and I was proud.

On one of our exercise days, I moved my right index finger.

"Most people see what is, and never what can be"
-Albert Einstein

Sarah Todd

My ninth birthday, October 11th, was coming up, and I was so excited! My mom and I decided to celebrate with a sleepover party. I loved sleepovers!

On October 8th, I had my party. Before my guests came, I prepared the table, setting out plates, napkins, plastic silverware and party hats at each spot. When the guests finally arrived, we made and ate our own pizzas and decorated cupcakes! I chose vanilla cupcakes, decorated with pink and blue icing. However, I decided not to eat one of my cupcakes at my party, but I did get to have one the next day.

After we were finished eating, we went down to the basement to watch the movie, *Annie*. Unfortunately, about halfway through the movie we had to stop it because nobody was paying attention! We decided to just talk instead.

Those girls are so rowdy! And crazy! I thought. In a good way, though. There was no way I could say I wasn't! I mean, Sarah Todd is a crazy one!

Anyway, we stayed up pretty much all night, just playing! It was so fun! Well, not for my mom, of course, but I didn't want it to end!

Later, much to my mom's relief, we fell asleep for the last three hours or so of the night.

> "He that is down needs fear not fall"
>
> -John Bunyan

Jennifer

I did it! That little wiggle I got out of my finger was full of hope! Well, actually, when I say wiggle, I mean more of a twitch. Whatever it's called, it seemed worth a party! I kept twitching it over and over again, afraid that if I didn't I would lose it again.

My mom wasn't home at that time. She had gone out shopping with her cousin. I texted her, though, and she responded right away wanting a video! I tried to take it with my phone and text it to her, but the video was such bad quality she couldn't tell what was happening. She would be home later, though, to see it herself.

"Champions are made from something they have deep inside them- a desire, a dream, a vision"

a vision"

-Muhammed Ali

Sarah Todd

I woke up at about 7:30 the next morning, quickly realizing that I was the first one awake. I woke all my friends, and we talked for a few minutes before I finally got everyone upstairs. We ate Publix glazed doughnuts for breakfast, which I had specifically asked my mom for. We talked while we ate, and had a good breakfast. After everyone was finished, we played with my McDonald's drive-through toy, and alternated between being the cashier and the customer. During the game, my friends made such a big mess, and I ended up having to clean everything up by myself afterward!

After that, we all played the card game "UNO". I had a card holder with four different rows to fit about four to five different cards in each row, which made it easier to hold cards during card games. I used that to play Uno with my friends. I was having so much fun, and was trying not to remind myself that all my friends would have to be picked up at 9:30. I didn't want 9:30 to come!

Jennifer

The therapy was becoming too much. My mom had to drive me to three different places four times a week for therapy. So, my parents decided to look into a rehab facility for me to go to a couple hours a day, two times a week.

We decided to get me evaluated for a rehab institution that we had heard was really, really good. We went in to get evaluated one day, and the guy there said that he thought that I definitely needed the day long therapy, and it would be good for us to have it all at one place. Of course, this wouldn't end up exactly the way we had expected. But why should it?

Sarah Todd

We didn't even get to finish the UNO game because those girls were just too loud! So, I put the UNO stuff away, and my friends and I played in the basement. Some girls had to leave a little early, so the rest of us helped them clean up their overnight items. After a few girls left around eight o'clock, the rest of us went back down to the basement and hopped on an old blanket. One girl decided to take hold of the blanket and drag it around the basement! The girl pulling us was very tall, and strong. The rest of us held the edges of the soft, old blanket with all our might, as if we were going to fall down a deep cliff. We moved so fast that it felt like we were almost going to fall right out of the blanket!

"Woo hoo! This is fun!" we shouted. We did this for nearly an hour! Finally, though, the fun had to come to an end as we cleaned up all of the girly sleeping bags, pillows, toothbrushes, and toothpastes. The doorbell suddenly began to ring, and it kept ringing until all of my friends were gone. I thanked them all for coming as they left, and later thanked my mom for the party.

"It was so fun! Thank you!" I said to her with a big smile.

"You're welcome, Sweetie."

"Not failure, but low aim, is crime"

-James Russel Lowell

Jennifer

It was conference time at school. My mom drove us over to the school, and we walked inside, me leading the way to the eighth grade hallway.

We grabbed my folder, thick with papers. We sat down at a table and I quietly went through the papers and told my mom about each one. When I was done with that, we put the little flags with each teacher's name up. My math teacher came over and talked about all the normal things, like how good I was in class and all that. My English teacher came over and said the same things, and so did my history and science teachers. My Spanish teacher came over pretending to be running, because she was running the Chicago Marathon that weekend with my mom. Conference time had always been fun to me, and this was no exception.

My mom explained to all of them that I would be going to the rehab institution every Tuesdays and Thursdays from third period until the end of the school day. This didn't affect my history and science teachers, because I had them first and second periods, but I would miss my choir, English, Spanish, and math classes on those days.

The teachers all said that it sounded like a great plan, and it would be good for me to do my therapy during the day instead of smushed in between school and sleep. They all said I could go before school, after school, or during eighth grade gym class (my free period) to make up the work.

We left the conferences feeling very satisfied.

Sarah Todd

I had so much fun at my party! The minute everyone left, I wished that it wasn't over already.

Luckily, though, I had more sleepovers to look forward to, because I was going to sleep over at my grandma's house the next weekend!

My grandma, Katie (who we just call "Katie"), and my grandpa, whose name is Alex but is called Dede because that's what my brother called him as a baby, live around twenty minutes from where I do. That is a major bonus, because my dad's parents, who we call Gran and Grandad, live in a different state! Sadly, I don't get to see them very often.

Anyway, I was very excited. After my amazing party all I had to do was get through one more week of the same old, same old.

I went to her house that next Friday night, and came home Saturday after-noon. We had so much fun! She has a dog named Pekoe who is a Chinese Pekingese doggy. I loved to play with him, and he got so excited when I came over. I ended up having so much fun at the sleepover, but my birthday was over. I was happy that I was officially nine, though! Yay!

"Life is like a box of chocolates. You never know what you're gonna get"

-Forrest Gump

Jennifer

The Chicago marathon. My mom was running it with her friends, and I wanted to go and watch. Her cousin, Val, ended up taking me. I woke up early, got dressed quickly, ate some food, and waited for my ride.

We drove over to the train station and found a place to park before waiting for the train. It came, and we hopped on and grabbed our seats before handing our tickets to the conductor to be hole punched.

The train ride wasn't too bad. It was just enough time to feel worthwhile, but not too long. We exited the train at our stop and made our way out of the crowded station. We began the walk to our destination. It wasn't going to be very long, but it was a hot day, and I still got exhausted fairly easily, so it felt long.

We got over to where my mom was going to be ending and held up our signs. When she and her friends finally crossed the finish line, we yelled to them, but they didn't see us until afterward. Oh, well. It was fun anyway!

My mom and her friends went back to their hotel to shower and change, and we all met each other after to go home. We all piled into one of my mom's friend's car, and went through a drive-thru to get some food. Then we drove home, the adults talking about the experience. I promised myself that someday, I would be able to experience the same thing.

Sarah Todd

My mom had surprised me on my birthday, which was not too long after the party we had put together with my friends, with two front row tickets to see Toy Story 3 on ice! I was so excited! My mom had just taken me to see the movie version, which had just come out, and I thought it was so hilarious. I just couldn't wait! It was such a great birthday present.

Finally, the time came to go see the show. When we arrived, my mom bought me cotton candy to eat during the show. I enjoyed it very much, even though my hands got very sticky, and had a great time. They had all the characters from the movie, and the costumes looked very realistic. That movie had probably been my favorite in the series, mostly because I found it to be the funniest and the cutest. It was a great treat to get to do that with my mommy.

However, although I had an excellent time doing that, the fun, sadly, would not be able to last long. Only two days later, on October 17th, Mommy, Daddy, and I would travel for a two-week long trip to Baltimore, Maryland to Johns Hopkins medical center and the Kennedy Krieger Institute for different types of therapy and for different opinions on my condition. I could tell right from the start that those two weeks were not going to be very easy.

Jennifer

The night before my first day at the rehab institution I started making a card for my PT, the therapist I thought I would miss the most. The card was hard and time consuming, but fun! By now, my left hand was pretty strong, or at least strong enough to look, and even feel, normal. By now, I could move the index finger on my right hand more than just a twitch, and I could move my thumb about the same.

Sadly, I didn't have time to finish the card before I was tired enough to go to bed. I folded the card up and set it into my card box for safe-keeping. I got my pjs on, brushed my teeth, and hopped into bed.

The next day was just like every other. I didn't have go to school for some reason, so I slept in, then woke up, ate something, got dressed into a tank-top per my mom's request so the therapists could see my shoulder, then packed up my iPad and a couple snacks and waited for my ride.

Neither of my parents could take me, so one of our family's best friends, Cathy, was going to.

The car ride was fairly long, and it was the middle of the day. The sunlight was soft, warm, and calming, and it took everything in me to stay awake.

When we arrived at the facility, a lady at the front desk greeted us, and we filled out a little bit of paperwork. Then we were shown around the place, and finally left at the cafeteria with only a list telling me who I was going to see, when, and where.

Sarah Todd

The day after the Toy Story 3 on ice performance, my mom and I began packing, along with my dad. My dad was coming with us, but my grandma could only stay with my brothers for three days, so my dad went home twice during the trip, and came back twice.

Anyway, I honestly really didn't know what was going to happen at Kennedy Krieger. All I knew was that I was going to see a PT and an OT. I would also see many doctors there. Ugh! I wasn't looking forward to that part, but I was quite excited to go on an airplane for my first time! I could tell it was going to be quite an adventure!

That day came. The big day. My parents and I gathered all of our things- bags, purses, etc.- and loaded them into the van. My grandma arrived to stay with my brothers, and then we all said our goodbyes and thanked her for staying with Alex and John. I hugged Katie, John, and even Alex (briefly...), and we got into the car. I noticed John's face was red, and so was Katie's. Of course Alex's wasn't; he was too cool to cry! My mom and I bawled practically the whole way to the airport. I could tell my dad was pretty sad, too, but he had to focus on the road. After an hour-long drive we finally arrived. I could see many airplanes taking off, but noticed that there were mostly Delta, because they're based in Atlanta. That was the airline we were about to go on. We found a parking place on the huge deck, grabbed our things, and walked inside. It was so loud at the airport, I could hardly hear what my parents were saying!

As soon as we got inside I noticed that there were people everywhere, either checking their bags, in security, or getting their tickets at the self-paying machines. We checked our bag first and then walked through security. It took forever! The line was so long, and moving so slow. Finally, after 20 minutes of waiting, and taking shoes off, walking either barefoot or in socks on the airport floor, which was gross, we made it through! At least we saved ourselves enough time, so we weren't late. After security, we sat on a bench and took a restroom break. Then, we went down a long escalator to a big train, an underground train that took us to our gate. I was so scared!

I boarded the train with my parents, and we found a seat for me, because I couldn't stand and hold onto the railing, of course. I made it through to gate B, and even though I was a little scared, it was kind of fun! After we arrived, we had a little extra time before we had to be at our gate, so we got a little snack out of a machine. I had a bag of red Doritos and Sprite. My parents had mini sandwiches. After we grabbed our snacks we sat at our gate. We ate while we waited, and I saved some food for the flight.

Finally, I heard the lady standing at the desk call first class and anyone who needed special assistance boarding to come aboard. We waited, and boarded at Zone 3. The lady scanned our tickets and we walked down the long jet way.

On the plane my mom and I sat together, while my dad sat across from us. I got the window seat, since I wanted to see outside once the plane took off. Pretty soon, the pilot started talking on the intercom, and said we were going to take off soon. I heard the engines starting, and we drove through the runway. Seconds later, we were in the air.

"Do not anticipate trouble, or worry about what may never happen. Keep in the sunlight"

-Benjamin Franklin

Jennifer

A lady came in telling me that she would be my PT during my days in day-rehab. We followed her into a room, where questions were asked and answered and I was evaluated. Then we walked over to a big gym, where I did many different exercises and activities. During one of them I stood on a trampoline while playing catch with the therapist. I stood on two legs at first, then did one at a time. I was amazed at how good I was able to balance after not being able to walk a couple months earlier. Afterward, I was introduced to an obstacle course that I had to walk through with a light backpack on.

I walked through the doors of the facility with the PT right beside me. The crisp, early autumn air felt welcoming, and I wasn't at all scared for our next activity. The PT was just going to have me walk on different surfaces like grass, pavement, and pebbles, to see if there were any difficulties. There weren't. Walking on different surfaces was no stranger after running on them in cross country just the year before.

We went back inside and returned to the cafeteria, where I would have a quick break before meeting with the OT. I only hoped it would be more challenging than PT had been.

Cathy and I played tic-tac-toe on my iPad in the cafeteria before the OT came to pick us up.

"Did you do that with your right hand?" the OT asked when she saw the game.

"No," I said honestly.

"I want you to do everything you can with your right hand."

On the outside, I smiled and nodded. On the inside, though, I sighed at the realization that this journey would be a lot harder than I ever would have expected.

I got up and followed her out the cafeteria doors. Cathy followed close behind me. We entered the small room the OT worked in and all sat down, Cathy in a chair by the door, and the therapist and I on opposite sides of a desk.

Right away, I knew I would like this therapist. She was extremely nice, just like the PT, and had an overall personality I really enjoyed. We talked, joked, and even laughed as she evaluated me and had me do different exercises.

She measured my finger and hand strengths and my range of motion first. Then I did different activities including putting little metal rods in different holes and closing my eyes as she placed an object in my hand and I tried to guess it. Most of these things used my right hand. At the end, the OT asked me if I could put my index finger and thumb together on my right hand. I took the flexible, navy blue thumb brace I had gotten shortly after school started off and attempted the seemingly impossible task she had just proposed. Slowly, I pinched my fingers together.

"If you can't figure out your purpose, figure out your passion. For your passion will lead you right into your purpose"

-Bishop T.D. Jakes

Sarah Todd

For the first few minutes of the plane ride, I entertained myself by looking out the window at the tiny world below, but after a little while it wasn't too exciting anymore. I was a little bored, but at least I wasn't scared! Still, I couldn't wait for the flight to be over so I could go to our hotel and lie down in a nice, comfy bed.

I was happy when our plane finally landed. We all got off and walked down a long jet way again. We walked into the Baltimore airport and I realized it was so quiet compared to the one in Atlanta! Hardly anybody was there!

We walked down to the baggage claim and waited FOREVER for our bags, close to thirty minutes! While we were waiting, I listened to two girls talking in front of us, and they sounded very country. I thought that what they said, in the best country accent ever, was pretty funny!

"I'm always relieved when I see my bag!" One girl said to the other. Now, imagine that in a country accent!

After we finally got our bag, my mom and I waited for my dad to go get a rental car. He finally arrived, and we hopped in, and on the way I listened to my parents figuring out the way to the "Homewood Suites" we were staying at.

> "Every great dream begins with a dreamer. Always remember, you have within you the strength, the patience, and the passion to reach for the stars to change the world"
>
> -Harriet Tubman

The tips of the index finger and thumb on my right hand touched. I was so happy! The OT then asked me to pinch my thumb and middle fingers together. I couldn't do it, but I already knew that. However, the OT had a challenge for me.

"I want you to keep working on getting those next fingers together. Once you have that, I want you to try to touch your thumb to your ring finger. Once you can do that, I want you to try your pinky."

I nodded, knowing it would be hard, but probably not impossible. As long as I kept working on it, that is. After all, the reason that finger is called an "opposable thumb" is because it can touch all of the other fingers, right to the tips.

Sarah Todd

After we arrived at the hotel, my parents and I went to dinner at a restaurant, then went back to our room in the hotel and relaxed before finally going to bed. The next morning we woke up super early to go to KKI.

Throughout the whole trip I had ten days of therapy at KKI, which totaled around twenty hours of OT in the gym, six hours of OT in the pool, and ten hours of PT in the gym. I also had a doctor appointment with Dr. Becker, a Transverse Myelitis expert, and a neuro-surgeon, meaning he tried to find well-working nerves to move to a different place in the body with nerves that don't work well. When we saw him he didn't find any ideas for me just by doing a muscle test, which is where he asked me to move different muscles to see how strong they were. He ordered an EMG (Electromyography) test, which was very painful because the doctor used needles and put them in different muscles and asked me to move that muscle while the needle is in the muscle which, seriously, does not work at all! Trust me, it hurts super bad.

After it was over, I was so relieved, and the nurse gave me five lollipops... Seriously nurse? That's it? You should have given me five hundred dollars for going through that! Well, I knew that wasn't going to happen. But a girl could dream.

Anyway, after all that nonsense the neuro-surgeon didn't have any ideas for nerve transfers.

So, that wraps up my Baltimore trip! Sound fun?

"Even if I knew that tomorrow the world would go to pieces, I would still plant my apple tree"

- Martin Luther

Jennifer

I got back from day rehab absolutely exhausted. It had been a really long, confusing day, but I knew that every time I went to the rehab institution the experience would get better. I knew I would get to be more familiar with the people and environment.

That night felt refreshingly normal. When I got home from the rehab facility I read a book and relaxed. I ate dinner, then did my homework, and went to bed on time. I was so excited to not have to do any therapy in the evening! I had the whole afternoon to myself, or it at least felt like it. And I liked that.

Sarah Todd

That November, my parents and I went to Birmingham, Alabama to see a Neurological Disease specialist who specializes mostly for Multiple Sclerosis, which is similar to TM. We drove to Birmingham and back in one day, and it was a long day. I had blood drawn when I was there, too, and the nurse doing it was horrible at it!

Then, that December, my parents and I went to Philadelphia, Pennsylvania by airplane to see two doctors who both did tendon transfers, which are similar to nerve transfers, but with tendons instead of nerves. They both had an idea involving my lungs, but we decided not to do it because my lungs weren't very strong. We planned to go back and see them later for more ideas.

"First say to yourself what you would be;

and then do what you have to do"

-Epictetus

Jennifer

Unfortunately, the therapy-free evenings were not going to last.

According to the rehab institution, I didn't need as much therapy time as my parents and I thought. They decided I was well enough to cut my four hours a week down to two hours. It was actually a fairly long drive to get there, and I would still be missing quite a bit of school even when it was cut down, so my parents decided it wasn't worth all that for two hours of therapy a week.

Part of me was sad that I would have to go back to the crammed schedule. Part of me was annoyed at the rehab institution for thinking I needed a limited amount of therapy. Part of me, though, was happy to go back to my nice, understanding, fun therapists I had already grown used to.

"You don't have to see the whole staircase, just take the first step"

- Martin Luther King, Jr.

Sarah Todd

January finally came along, after a wonderful Christmas! Since I live in Georgia, we don't really expect snow that often. But in January 2011, we had snow! Snow in Georgia? Very surprising, I know.

My dad and I went outside and attempted to build a snowman, which was obviously difficult for me. I could really only pick up a tiny bit of snow at a time to add onto the snowman. We also tried having snowball fights with my brothers. My mom stood by and watched, and I actually picked up a small ball of snow, and threw it! After a long day of playing in the snow, and my brothers trying to convince me to sled, which didn't happen, we went inside and got hot cocoa. My mom helped me change out of my wet jeans, and we laid them over the heater to dry.

Of course, I have my dog, Buddy, who is very curious and mischievous! While we were all watching tv, Buddy crept up towards my jeans on the heater. He was scared of them! It was quite funny to watch! Sometimes he would back up because they startled him. Silly dog! My family and I, including Buddy, had a wonderful snow day.

Jennifer

We all know that Transverse Myelitis is rare, right? Most people in the world haven't heard of it. I mean, if you walked up to some random person and asked them if they knew what Transverse Myelitis is, chances are they would stare at you blankly and walk away. However, even before I was diagnosed with it, one of my mom's friends asked her on Facebook if she had ever heard of "Transverse Myelitis", because my symptoms seemed to match up to it. That, alone, is pretty coincidental.

Probably one of the weirdest things that had to do with TM, though, actually happened a couple months after my family was introduced to it. By that time, I had started to think of those words to sum up my life.

Sarah Todd

Since Valentine's Day was coming soon, my mom decided that it would be fun to let me have a few friends over for a Valentine's party. We planned many fun activities like decorating cookies, playing games, and decorating Valentine bags. For party favors, I gave each girl a pretty notebook. I only invited three people but we still had fun.

After all the fun was over it was time for my mom and I to go to Baltimore again. My dad didn't go this time; he stayed at home with my brothers while mom and I stayed for two weeks.

For the third time ever, we went on a plane together. We stayed at the Homewood Suites again, like last time. At the gym I saw the same two therapists.

One day after I finished PT my mom introduced me to a woman named Kim and her daughter Annie. My mom and I learned that Annie also had Transverse Myelitis, and was affected from the waist-down. Annie was 14 years old at the time we met her. Annie and Mrs. Kim were also staying at the same hotel as us, so we decided that when we were finished at KKI we would meet up for dinner. We did, and Annie and I hung out. It was really fun!

That second Baltimore trip was way better than the first, considering that I didn't have any painful tests, I already knew the therapists, I was familiar with the place, and I had a friend to hang out with.

Jennifer

I saw many different doctors and specialists after being diagnosed with TM. Besides the obvious- neurologist, physical therapist, and occupational therapist- I went to an ophthalmologist, a neuro ophthalmologist, rheumatologist, cardiologist, urologist, gastroenterologist, neuro-psychologist, lipids clinic, neurovascular doctor, endocrinologist, thrombophilia clinic, and podiatrist. A couple of these were from before, but the majority I had to see as a result of Transverse Myelitis. Many people with TM have a similar list.

With all those doctors came many different nurses, and I realized that many of them enjoyed telling stories. Most of them didn't stick with me at all, but one doctor's nurse's story will probably be remembered for a long time. This is because it was about Transverse Myelitis. As it turns out, it had already been a part of her life.

Sarah Todd

April was not the most exciting month for me, except that I got my ears pierced! I was a little scared at first, but after I got it done I was very pleased.

Then in May I fell on tile and scraped my chin. Because my arms didn't work well, I couldn't catch myself to keep that from happening. So, I had to go to the hospital to get stitches.

On a happier note, it was also my school's third grade field trip in May, where we went to Dahlonega and went gold mining. We got to go underground and see the gold mines. It was very fun, and I got to keep some gems that I found!

All my friends were so excited to see me. It had been such a long time. It was very fun to get to catch up with all of them. I had a lot of fun talking to them on the bus. I was glad that I didn't totally miss out on my third grade year!

Jennifer

"Did you say Transverse Myelitis?" The nurse asked after my mom told her I had it. We both nodded.

"Oh my gosh!" she said enthusiastically, "My son had that! He was only affected in the legs, though."

"Yeah," my mom said, "we have yet to find someone else affected in the arms, too."

"Oh, ok. It's hard, isn't it?" the nurse asked before talking about her son and his symptoms and all that. I started to zone most of it out, since I could tell she would be talking about it for a while, until I heard, "...sadly, though, he passed away..."

What? I sat up, alarmed, and the nurse noticed.

"It wasn't from TM, though; it was something totally different. But it's so weird how it's a very rare disease, yet somehow we met each other!"

My mom and I both kind of nodded at that, and the nurse kept talking. And talking. And talking. I wasn't thinking about any of this, though. Instead, I was thinking of that nurse's son, and wishing badly that I could meet someone else with it, someone who understood.

"We can't live in the light all of the time. You have to take whatever light you can hold into the darkness with you"

-Libba Bray

Sarah Todd

It was the end of the school year. I finished 3rd grade! My parents couldn't believe that I learned everything I needed to just by having school two days a week for an hour and a half each time. Only three hours a week!

I really wanted to go back to real school for 4th grade, though, because I missed out on lunchtime with my friends, recess, fun school activities, and different ways of learning. Unlike other kids, I always really enjoyed school. I was also always a big grammar freak! If somebody said a sentence grammatically incorrect, I always had to correct them.

Even though I wanted to go back to school for fourth grade, I had a great 3rd grade year with wonderful Ms. Stewart.

Jennifer

The nurse, the one who was talking forever about her son with TM, wrapped up the story-telling and started praying. It was so deep and heart-touching that I couldn't keep tears from sliding down my face. I looked over at my mom and saw that she was having the same problem.

When she finished, we said our goodbyes, and as I walked over to the car with my mom I asked myself why I had cried at that particular prayer, and not the million others I had heard throughout my life. Deep-down, I already knew the answer, though. This lady, a total stranger whom I had never met before, knew the pain we were going through. She not only knew it but embraced it, cared for us, and made sure we knew it through her kind words and actions.

Sarah Todd

I had a really fun summer, and it was now time for 4th grade! My mom went to many meetings over the summer to figure out how I would go to school, and I had to complete many tests at school to be able to attend school again. My mom and the principal came to the conclusion that I would have a full time aide to help me do whatever I needed. I also would leave 45 minutes early because I wouldn't do art, music, P.E., or Health. So, the principal scheduled those activities for the end of the day.

I was very nervous for the first day of school, but also couldn't wait, and we decided that my mom would drive me to school every morning a little later than the other kids arrived. I also got lucky enough to have Ms. Stewart be my 4th grade teacher! She moved up from 3rd grade to 4th grade! That was a big plus. I could tell that Ms. Stewart, my aide, and the principal were going to make this a good year.

Jennifer

I was finally done with the Prednisone! I had been sent home from the hospital with pills of it, and a few weeks later I took my last dose in triumph. Even though I didn't have any more hallucinations from it, there were other side-effects that were driving me crazy. One was that it never allowed me to feel full. Eating extra didn't bother me because I was skinny in the first place, and lost a ton of weight after getting sick, but I couldn't stand never feeling full.

Another side-effect was a puffy face. For an almost 14-year-old, that was the worst! That, unfortunately, didn't go away right after my last dose of Prednisone. It took a long time for it to completely wear off, and it wore off gradually. My face was still puffy when it came time for school pictures.

The morning of school pictures I wore my nicest, picture-friendly clothes and my mom crimped my hair. When I got to school we found out that the eighth graders were scheduled to get their pictures done after lunch, so we excitedly went through the motions all morning until the time came. When it did, we headed down to the multipurpose room and, one by one, got our pictures taken.

A couple weeks later we got our pictures back. By then my puffiness was considerably lower, and I could definitely tell a difference in my school picture. It was definitely not my favorite picture of myself, but at least my smile looked good...

> "You are unique, and if that is not fulfilled,
> then something has been lost."
> - Martha Graham

Sarah Todd

My parents and I learned that having therapy sessions in the pool was beneficial. So, my dad had the idea to put our very own pool in the backyard! After discussing it multiple times, we all agreed to get a pool. We could use it for therapy and for fun.

We found a pool company, picked out tiles, and designed it. After many months of removing trees, digging, and getting the shape right, it was finished. We filled it up with water from our hose, and started to heat it up.

I never had to go to the YMCA or Swim Atlanta for pool therapy with my PT anymore. Instead, I went to my backyard.

Jennifer

My nails had, for whatever reason, been my biggest frustration my whole life. I hated them too long and I hated them too short. When I was little I dreaded nail trimming days and literally cried every time, except when my mom painted them right afterward. I was a strange child.

Anyway, I was incredibly annoyed that I couldn't clip my fingernails myself after I got TM. My mom did it a couple times, but then decided one day to bring me to get a manicure. She figured that if someone else was going to do it, it might as well be fun.

So, we went to a salon that was close by to do just that.

We waited for a couple minutes until they were ready, because they were pretty busy. Finally, a lady called me over to begin. She soaked my hands, moisturized them, trimmed and filed the nails. Then she trimmed my cuticles, causing me to almost cry out in pain. Dumb nerve pains.

When she was done with that I rinsed my hands, then I handed her the color I picked out and she started painting my nails. She started with my left, first layering on the clear coat. Then she moved onto my right.

"Keep your fingers straight."

She repeated this over and over again when she worked on my right hand. Every time I tried but, of course, I couldn't. And since she didn't seem to speak much English, I was pretty sure she wouldn't understand if I tried to explain.

Finally, she got very frustrated.

"I have a lot of people waiting and if you mess up your nails by not keeping your fingers straight I'm not doing them over!"

"I can't...." I said, annoyed, in my mind.

I wished I could really scream it at her, but I couldn't. I just sat there, mad at Transverse Myelitis and her for being so rude, and continuously apologized for smudging her precious nail art.

Sarah Todd

October came, and I turned 10! I became double digits. I went out with my grandparents and my family to Bonefish that evening for dinner. I also had a sleepover party with a few friends, and my family gave me some presents.

For more fun, mom found a camp for chronically ill children called "Victory Junction". They were doing a three day camp for kids with TM, so we applied, and got in to go. I was excited, because a girl who had TM named Lindsay was going, too, and she was seven.

My grandma stayed with my brothers, while my mom and dad went with me. At the camp, they had a gym, a walk-through maze, mini golf, an arts and crafts building, a huge stage (which had dressing rooms, a backstage, and seats), an ice cream shop, a pool (it was too cold to swim, though, since it was October!), a tree house, horseback riding, an outdoor stage, zip lining, and cabins. In each cabin, there were two bedrooms, with a family room in-between, so there were two families total in each cabin.

Every morning there would be a breakfast, then we would have free-time. After free-time we ate lunch, and after lunch they showed a movie on the stage. Then it was free-time until dinner. Each day was tiring, but very fun! Lindsay and I did two acts for the talent show they hosted. In one, I said the woodchuck, and in the second one we did an act called "The Crazy Girls". Our second act cracked everybody up! Lindsay and I totally had an amazing time.

I met another person with TM, too. Her name was Erica. She was affected waist down, unlike me. Her younger brother, Justin, who's a year older than me, hung out with me, too. Erica and Justin became good friends of mine, and our moms became good friends, as well.

"Ask yourself: 'Can I give more?'. The answer is usually: 'Yes'."

-Paul Tergat

Jennifer

"Reese, come on!" I said as I approached my 7th grade brother at his locker at the end of the school day. He said he was coming as he continued to shove stuff in his backpack.

Suddenly, one of his friends walked over.

"What'd you do to your hand?" He asked, eyeing my brace. I sighed. The same thing had come out of many mouths during the school year.

"She had a spinal cord injury," my brother said vaguely, "so she can't move it."

"Oh," he said, "are you a cripple?"

"Uhhhh," I said, not sure how to respond.

"Cripple! You're a cripple! Ha!" He said a couple times. I just rolled my eyes. He didn't mean to annoy me, I knew that. He just sincerely thought he was making a hilarious joke.

"Dude, stop that," Reese said, not amused at all. His friend stopped that day, but for the rest of the year when he saw me in the halls he would ask if I was still crippled.

Sarah Todd

Halloween was very fun in 2011. I dressed up as Cinderella in her rags. It was a lovely costume that my grandma Katie worked hard to make. All my neighbors thought that I looked adorable. I kept getting so many compliments on my dress.

It was very cold outside, and my annoying nerve pains were making my hands go numb. I could hardly move my right hand, and my left hand hurt badly. Since I could barely hold a heavy bag of candy, I carried a bucket and when it got full, my mom emptied all the candy from it into a pillow case she was carrying. That way, I didn't have to carry around a heavy bucket of candy. Of course, my brothers got way more candy than I did, though, because their hands didn't freeze up. But by the end of the night, I was tired, cold, and had a lot of candy!

"The miracle isn't that I finished. The miracle is that I had the courage to start."

-John Bingham

Jennifer

Late fall of 2011 brought many fun things. One in October was the Halloween dance at school. At first I was worried about getting tired during it and wanting to go home, especially since it was starting right after physical therapy. But I had fun, and wasn't exhausted or uncomfortable at all. That was new to me, but very nice. Shortly after that came Halloween itself, which proved to be equally fun.

When November came it brought my fourteenth birthday. I was so excited! I was already technically a teenager, but fourteen seemed more teen-ish than thirteen to me. Plus, thirteen had brought TM. I was sure that fourteen would be an age filled only with improving.

Fall 2011 also brought something that I had been begging for for a long time. A Facebook! My mom finally allowed me to have an account, mostly wanting me to connect with other people with TM who's moms she'd been talking to and getting to know for a while.

The first girl I talked to with TM was Erica. We messaged a couple times and I found that she was my age and affected waist-down. My lesions on my spine were very high (pretty much as high as you can go), and hers were very low. Still, we had a couple good conversations, and then she said that she knew some other girls with TM. She told me she would "recommend" them to me on Facebook. I was excited!

A couple days later a notification popped up on my account. I clicked on it, and it read, "Sarah Todd Hammer. Suggested by Erica". Next to it were two buttons, which said "add friend" and "ignore".

I clicked "add friend" and waited to see if she would accept me.

Part

3

A Growing Friendship

"We either make ourselves miserable, or we make ourselves strong.

The amount of work is the same."

- Carlos Castaneda

Sarah Todd

John made me a Facebook account so that I could talk to my friends. One day, I was on Facebook, and I noticed that I had a friend request. It said that it was "suggested by Erica" and that the person's name was "Jen Starzec". I had no clue who this person was, so I clicked decline. Then, the next time I was on Facebook, I had another friend request from Jen Starzec. I decided to accept it, figuring she had TM because Erica suggested her, and send her a message since I didn't know who she was. So, I sent: "??", asking who she was, without giving any information about myself. I wondered what her response would be.

After I sent that request I almost completely forgot about it. That is, until she accepted.

I scrolled through Facebook one day, noticing that I had a new notification and message. The notification said that Sarah Todd Hammer had accepted my friend request. I smiled. I couldn't wait to talk to another girl with TM!

I opened up the message.

"??"

I thought for a second, not sure how to respond to that without giving too much information about myself, since I didn't know her. I asked my mom, who was sitting next to me, and gathered some ideas. Hesitantly, I started to type.

Our Facebook messages from November, 2011...

Sarah Todd Hammer:

??

Jen Starzec:

You were recommended by Erica W. Do you have TM too? I was diagnosed 8/16/11. My arms were mostly affected. Erica said she would suggest other TM girls. I'm 14.

Sarah Todd Hammer:

Ohhh okay. Yes I do. My whole body was affected but now my arms are. I'm 10. I got mine 4/19/10

Jen Starzec:

My whole body was affected too, but I was able to walk pretty quickly. Now it's mostly my arms (right fingers and wrist are way weaker), and now I'm learning to write with my left hand for things that don't require much writing and my iPad for longer things. Do you have a way to handwrite and stuff?

Sarah Todd Hammer:

Yes. You're kind of opposite!! I could walk pretty quickly but my left hand doesn't move at all... My right hand works but not fully... I am a righty, but my left shoulder works better than my right shoulder!!!

Jen Starzec:

Oh, ok!

Sarah Todd

Of course, I love to dance. I always dance to my DVDs from my old dance company. I'm in many of them!

In my basement I have a fake stage and a huge rack of costumes. I've always loved make-up, and I have a huge basket filled with it.

In my room, I have a pink Disney Princess vanity. It was a birthday present from my mommy when I turned six.

I used to dance upstairs in my mom and dad's room with their TV, but now I dance in the family room with the big TV.

Props are very fun to use while dancing. I love to make my own props, and find stuff around the house that's similar to the props in my DVDs. Same with costumes, I used to use my own clothes to have similar costumes, but now I use costumes that I get for Christmas or my birthday!

I have so many dance DVDs, probably about 50! I have all the dances on them memorized. Sometimes I add choreography to the dances in the videos. We have so many videos of me dressed up in costumes dancing to videos when I was younger. They are so cute!

My mom introduced me to dance, and now I do it all the time. I was born to dance!

Jennifer

December in Illinois brought two things: cold and snow. 2011 was no exception. The cold flared up my nerve pains a bit, although it wasn't nearly as bad this winter as it would later turn out to be in 2012-2013, but I always thought the snow was incredibly beautiful, especially when it covered the grass completely, like a sparkly, pure, soft blanket hiding the imperfections.

Most Decembers, like pretty much every month, were predictable. I mean, I'd lived fourteen of them by now! The cold air would begin early, a sign that snow was going to come. Then the first snowfall would come, and although Chicago-area winters were long, the first snowfall of winter never ceased to amaze me. After the first snowfall would hopefully come many, many others, and hopefully we would have a white Christmas. Usually we did.

This December really wasn't as predictable as most. Something happened that I probably won't forget for a long time, and probably won't experience ever again.

My mom is a therapist for babies who are blind and visually impaired. Some of these kids just have eye problems, which the kids often learn to adapt to. Others, however, have vision problems in addition to very serious medical problems.

One little girl she worked with had a condition where, in short, she slowly lost many motor skills as a baby. My mom worked with her until she turned three, which was the age she usually stops working with all her clients because that is when they start preschool. However, she continued to keep in touch with this family as she frequently tries to with her former clients.

After a doctor's appointment in downtown Chicago one day my mom told me that we were going to see an old client of hers, the little girl I mentioned earlier, because she was in the hospital with a bad case of pneumonia. When we arrived I realized it was the same hospital I had stayed in just four months earlier. When we walked in I was flooded with memories. It felt so weird to walk in as a visitor instead of a patient. I hadn't been there since I'd been discharged.

We checked in and then walked over to the little girl's room. This adorable four-year-old girl was covered in tubes and wires! Breathing tubes, feeding tubes, IV tubes... I just felt heartbroken.

My mom introduced me to the little girl's mom and two other ladies, apparently other therapists of the girl's, in the room. They were incredibly nice! After introducing us, my mom talked to her for a long time. I opened up the case to my iPad, which I had brought along, and pulled the iPad out. I found a little kid game, which I had gotten for my two-year-old sister, and carried my iPad over to the young girl. Her eyes lit up. She knew exactly what it was. I held the iPad out in front of her and helped her play the games until she got tired of them.

Since it was so close to Christmas, and all those other winter holidays, the hospital room was covered in decorations. There were decorated cardboard circles hanging by strings and balloons, amongst other things, which the little girl enjoyed playing with. She would rip the strings off the cardboard circles, making us all laugh, and liked holding on to and bouncing the balloons.

Most of the balloons in the room had little clips attached to the bottom to keep from flying away. The girl put her fingers around one balloon's clip, trying to pinch it open. It didn't work. Her condition had weakened her fingers greatly... like TM had done to mine.

Before I could even think I grabbed the balloon and shoved the clip into my right hand, pinching my fingers together as hard as I could. Nothing. The clip didn't move a millimeter.

"See," I said softly, "I can't do it either."

Too soon we had to leave. I said bye to the little girl, who had filled me with so much love. I went home with my iPad, a couple of the games now holding a lot of memories and meaning, and one of the cardboard circles she had ripped most of the string off of. I had written on it, "Prayers for" and then her name, and I hung it up in my room when I got home. She was special. Getting to visit her was more special than anyone knew or will ever know.

On December 25th I was just as excited as I had been every year before. I got a bunch of cool presents, although opening them had never been my favorite part. Walking downstairs to the tree early in the morning was my favorite part. It always felt magical.

This Christmas, though, I couldn't stop thinking of that little girl and her weakening condition. I told myself that I would give all those presents away if she would just get better. I kept picturing her covered in those tubes and wires and really hoped for a Christmas miracle. Even though she was obviously in a much more severe, serious situation than I'd ever been in in my life, I actually related to her a little bit. I wanted to meet someone with TM in person, but this was good enough for now. This was the start of something. I knew it.

"The journey between who you once were, and who you are now becoming, is where the dance of life really takes place."

- Barbara De Angelis

Sarah Todd

At Christmastime, we had a little party at school. Since I went to a public school, we had to call it a "Winter Party".

We played fun games and had yummy snacks. In one game, two of my friends had to wrap me up in toilet paper! It was hilarious! We also got to hang out with our friends. After the party, we were finally on our two week break!

When Christmas came, I was super excited! My grandparents and my uncle came for dinner on Christmas Eve, and we played the game "The Right Family". My grandma slept over in my room, and my uncle A.J. stayed at Katie's and Dede's house with Dede overnight. On Christmas morning, Dede and Uncle A.J. drove to my house, and my brothers and I opened presents from Santa. I gave my family their presents before I opened mine. I could never wait to see their reaction. After Christmas at my house, we went over to Katie's and Dede's house for more presents, and a wonderful Christmas dinner.

"It's supposed to be hard. If it wasn't hard, everyone would do it. The hard...is what makes it great!"

-Tom Hanks in *A League of Their Own*

Jennifer

I celebrated the New Year with practically my whole neighborhood. We gathered at my friend Sara's house on New Year's Eve, hanging out and keeping each other occupied until it was around 11:50 p.m. That was when we would watch the countdown on TV and wake up the rest of the neighborhood celebrating.

When the time finally came the adults got glasses of champagne and the rest of us got sparkling cider. Sara's mom passed out little blow horns. Waiting eagerly we shouted "FIVE... FOUR... THREE... TWO... ONE... HAPPY NEW YEAR!!!!"

Everyone dumped their drinks in their mouths and blew as hard as they could on the horns. We ran out into the backyard, ignoring the cold, and blew on the horns until the parents made us come back inside. We jumped up and down screaming "IT'S 2012!!!!!! IT'S 2012!!!!!!!"

Through all of this I realized something. 2011 was when my life was changed forever. Now that was over. I could turn a new leaf. The hardest part of my journey was gone. It was a brand new year, and was going to be my first full year with Transverse Myelitis. And my resolution was to make the best of it.

"Some men have thousands of reasons why they cannot do what they want to, when all they need is one reason why they can."

- Martha Graham

Sarah Todd

After our nice, long break, it was back to school for me. The spelling bee was going on, and I won for my class on the word "ladder". That was probably the easiest word to win on. Since I won, I got to compete in the spelling bee for the whole school against 5th graders. I kept getting word after word correct, but then it came to the word, "weasel". I spelled it, "W-E-A-S-L-E". So, I lost. I only had two letters switched around!

Overall, I came in 4th place. All the other 4th graders were out. So, I won for the whole 4th grade! I couldn't believe that I knocked out most of the 5th graders!

Anyway, after I lost, I could spell some of the words! They were easy, like "chorus" and "gallon". Ugh, it made me so mad. You can't win everything, though.

When the spelling bee was over, they served lemonade and cookies in the library, which was where the spelling bee was held. When I came back into the classroom, everyone cheered. The classrooms were able to watch the spelling bee on an Active Board, or a Smart Board. So, everyone was proud of me. My parents had come to watch me, too! It was a very fun experience for me.

Jennifer

"We're going to go to this hospital in Baltimore, Maryland that has doctors who specialize in Transverse Myelitis. It's called John's Hopkins."

When my mom told me this I didn't know whether to be excited, scared, or something else. I'd never been to Maryland, and I was always excited to go to different states. But I was also scared because I hated doctor's appointments and I would be going on my first plane ride since I was about 7.

The week before we left I wasted no time at all gathering homework from my teachers. I was going to miss a whole week of school being there, which I was pretty happy about!

The day before we left I said "goodbye" to my family about a million times. My dad was going to run the house while my mom stayed with me. I also said an early happy birthday to my little brother Bryce, since I would be missing it, February 16th, while I was in Baltimore. It was going to be his fifth birthday! I hoped I would get a chance to say "happy birthday" again over the phone. At least I would be home just in time for my sister Jolie's third birthday, though.

I packed and checked my suitcase a million times before going to bed. Early in the morning we were driven to the airport, and before I knew it I was on the plane. Luckily the ride wasn't too long. It was about an hour and a half.

We arrived in Baltimore, dropped our stuff off at where we were staying, which was the Children's House right by the John's Hopkins hospital, and decided to explore the city for the rest of the day. It was pretty fun!

The next day, though, wasn't quite as fun. I did a bunch of tests and saw quite a few doctors. One test I got was some eye test for some vision blurriness I had been experiencing for a little while. While I was in there my mom talked some things over with the neurologist I had just finished seeing.

Afterward we walked over to the Kennedy Krieger Institute for another random doctor appointment and a visit with an occupational therapist. The appointment was nothing exciting. The doctor asked a million questions and examined me, and the OT just gave us some extra pads to put on my night brace.

On the walk back I asked my mom what she and the neurologist had talked about while I was taking the vision test.

"Oh, just stuff. He looked at your MRIs," she said vaguely. I left it at that. We walked in silence for a little while.

"He thinks that you might not have Transverse Myelitis," she said, breaking the silence.

"He thinks you had a spinal cord stroke.

"To dance is to be out of yourself. Larger, more beautiful, more powerful"

- Agnes De Mille

Sarah Todd

One thing that I love to do is choreograph dances. I often choreograph dances to songs on my iPhone. That way, I can do all my favorite moves in the dance, including my "signature" moves.

Once I start choreographing a dance, I can't stop. I love it! I get my dances done usually within two days or so. Then, I show them to my mom, dad, and grandma Katie. They are always impressed. It's great to be able to do what I love and get compliments on it.

When I'm bored I always do a few of my dances, and then sometimes make up another one!

Also, I love to make up plays with my friends using my stage. We dress up and it's very fun.

Dance is really something that has changed my life. I'm so glad that I can do it, even with having TM.

Jennifer

For a second I was just shocked. But then I actually thought about it and burst into tears. I was finally getting used to the idea of having Transverse Myelitis... And now I was being hit with this?

My mom tried to console me, saying that he wasn't sure and we would have to do some tests, possibly including something called a spinal angiogram, to know more details. But that just made it worse.

"Why does everything keep changing?" I choked, and she just shook her head.

"I don't know."

The rest of the way back to the Children's House she tried explaining what he'd found on the MRI that made him think that, but I couldn't really listen. We got back and I flopped onto my bed, silent for the rest of the day.

The next two days were equally as fun. I had to do a two-day long, extensive neuropsychology test. This was because my mom and some teachers had noticed that, although I was still smart and worthy of my advanced classes, it was taking me much longer to get the answers. My mom scheduled the test to figure out what was up.

The test stressed me out. I got a break for lunch, and of course in between the two days I got to go back to our room, but that was about it. I gave the best answers I could, stressing out about the doctors thinking I wasn't as smart as I was. The tests ranged from math worksheets to solving world problems. The math worksheets and reading comprehension and stuff like that were incredibly easy, but the ones I had to explain were really hard.

Finally, it was done. My mom and I met with the doctor in her office for the results. Basically, she said I was very, very smart, but it took a long time to get there. She said it could be from the medicine I was on for my migraines, but probably not since I was on such a low dose. She said it was most likely from being distracted from writing with my left hand and repositioning myself a million times from my chronic nerve pains.

On our last day in Baltimore we met up with the neurologist for a little bit, and he told us that he wanted us to come back to do a spinal angiogram about a month later. Hoping it would cheer me up, we spent the rest of the day exploring Baltimore. We went to the mall and bought Baltimore t-shirts (I got a purple one for myself and a little pink one for my sister Jolie) and went to the aquarium.

In the end, we realized that although we had gone to Baltimore in hopes of getting answers, we were mostly left with more questions.

Sarah Todd

At school, the 4th graders got to do a Science Fair project. I decided to do "How Many Licks Does it Take to Get to the Center of a Tootsie Pop?" as mine. I licked a Tootsie Pop, and got my mom and dad to lick Tootsie Pops, too. We all ended up with different amounts of licks! My mom had around 700, my dad had around 500, and I had about 800. We figured that the amounts had to do with the tongue size. So, I took all three numbers and averaged them.

That was the hard part. The fun part was decorating my poster board and putting my observations on it! My mom helped me put it together, and we used three Tootsie Pops for the O's in "Tootsie Pop". I loved presenting my project in the gym, and I got an A on it.

"To get to the finish line, you'll have to try lots of different paths."

- Amby Burfoot

Jennifer

"When am I going to be able to run again?" I asked my mom for the millionth time since August sixteenth, 2011. Her answer every time was, "Hopefully soon, we have to talk to your therapist."

But this time, it was different. And I was pleasantly surprised!

"I was thinking... Maybe sometime this week you could go out for a run with your dad. A slow, short run. A mile at the most, and nothing faster than a 12 minute mile pace or so. And Dad would be a little behind you the whole time to watch your form."

My mouth practically dropped to the floor. It was like I was in a dream! I felt more excited than I'd been on Christmas!

I didn't mention it again for a couple days. Unfortunately, neither did my mom. Finally, in the middle of my math homework the evening of March 18th, 2012, my dad asked me if I wanted to go for a run.

As if 'no' was even an answer.

I bolted upstairs to my room and threw running shorts and a tank top on, per my mom's request so my dad could keep an eye on my shoulders. Luckily, it was a really warm evening.

I put on my shoes and my mom put my hair in a ponytail. I was so excited I was practically jumping up and down! My mom gave me her running watch so I could keep track of my pace and how far we were going, and then we were off.

"Be safe!" My mom called out the front door.

We went slow. Very slow. But it felt amazing. I paid attention to my breathing, the way it worked with my soft footsteps to create a pattern. The slight breeze plus the warm air made perfect running weather. It wasn't too humid or too dry, either. It was perfect.

Of course, Transverse Myelitis had to ruin the moment. For maybe an eighth of a mile I felt perfect, but sharp pains started shooting through my legs way too soon. The running was flaring my nerve pains. Luckily, I was a runner. Runners always have pains. Maybe not these types of pains, but they have pains. Over the years I learned to build up so much endurance, and I knew that without that, I wouldn't be where I was. I didn't let Transverse Myelitis beat me. I didn't let it win. I was always competitive, and TM was my biggest competitor. It hadn't beat me yet, and that wasn't about to change.

So I ignored the pain. I pushed through the pain. And the run was done much too quickly. I walked in the house feeling prouder and more accomplished than ever before.

After running upstairs to find my mom and excitedly tell her how great it had been, I went on Facebook to share the news.

"Finally got to run again! A slow mile, but... :)" I wrote. Immediately comments started showing up.

"Awesome! That was the best post I've read all day!"

"That's so exciting, I am so happy, go Jen!!"

"You go girl!!!!!!"

"Great news Jen! So happy for you!"

"Yay Jen!!!!!! That's awesome!!!!!!!!"

"Good job, Jen!"

I smiled. I could run. I COULD RUN! No matter what happened, no matter how much longer this journey was going to last, I knew that everything was going to be okay. Score 1 for Jen, 0 for Transverse Myelitis.

"The body says what words cannot."

- Martha Graham

Sarah Todd

My mom informed me that we would be going back to Baltimore soon. I wanted to know if any other people with TM were going at the same time as us. On Facebook there is a group called "Transverse Myelitis Teens" which has girls, including me, that have TM. So, I posted in the group, hoping someone would reply, "Is anyone going to Baltimore? I'm going on March 25."

A little later, Jen Starzec commented, "I'll be there that same week!"

I was immediately excited and hopped out of my chair to tell my mom. My mom was very happy, too, and talked to Jen's mom to arrange for us to meet each other. I had learned that Baltimore was way more fun with a friend after meeting Annie, so I was happy that I was going to meet another one.

When it was time for us to leave again for Baltimore, we flew on an airplane, and stayed at the Homewood Suites yet again.

Jennifer

Early March, 2012 I scrolled through the TM Teens Facebook group I had recently been added into, bored. All of a sudden, something caught my eye. Sarah Todd Hammer, the girl I had started Facebook messaging a few months before, had written, "Is anyone going to Baltimore? I'm going on March 25."

My first thought, naturally, was that my brother's birthday was on March 25th. But then I remembered something else. I was going to be in Baltimore that same week, because I had my spinal angiogram scheduled the 30th. Excitedly, I commented, and we both decided that we were going to have to find a time to meet each other.

A couple nights later I had a strange dream that Sarah Todd Hammer and I were standing on a very large map. "Come on!" She said, "Let's go to Connecticut!"

We hopped from where we were standing to that state and immediately appeared there. The next morning I told her about the "magic map" dream and she responded. "Cool! Well, we're going to Baltimore! Maybe we can hop there!"

I could tell that although she was four years younger than me, that girl and I were going to get along very well.

> "Success is getting what you want. Happiness is wanting what you get."
>
> - Dale Carnegie

Sarah Todd

On March 29, my mom told me that Jen and her mom were coming to visit us at our hotel. I was filled with excitement! During therapy all day I kept telling everybody that somebody else with TM was going to meet me. Everybody seemed very happy for me, and I couldn't wait.

When I was finished with therapy, my mom and I went back to the hotel, which we called "Homewood suite Homewood", and I waited forever. I didn't want to start doing something because I didn't know if Jen would arrive, and I wanted to be ready to meet her. My mom was texting Jen's mom, and Mrs. Starzec said that they would be over around 2:00, after they went to Whole Foods.

I played on my phone and waited patiently for them to arrive.

Jennifer

We arrived in Baltimore a couple weeks later. We went during spring break
this time so luckily I didn't have to bring any school work. When we got to where we
were staying, the Children's House again, it was night, so we went to bed right away.

When I woke up the next morning my mom told me the most exciting thing.

"At two o'clock today we are going to go meet Sarah Todd Hammer and her
mom at her hotel, then maybe go out for ice cream or dinner or something."

I got up and dressed and ready right away and impatiently jumped up and
down with excitement the whole morning. Finally, it was 1:30. My mom and I
hopped on the subway train and rode for about a minute to get to downtown Baltimore. We made it and shopped for a couple minutes before heading to their hotel.

We walked in, repeating the room number a couple times as we looked for it.
As it turns out, we didn't have to. We bumped into Mrs. Hammer, who was at the
vending machines, on our way there!

"Hi! It's so great to meet you guys!" She said after we introduced ourselves.
We followed her to her room and she swung the door open.

"Sarah Todd," she called. "Look who's here!"

Sarah Todd

Jen and Mrs. Starzec walked in, and my first thought when I saw Jen was, "She looks way different in person!"

We all sat down, my mom offered us drinks, and Jen and I smiled at each other. Our mothers began the oh so boring factual talk about TM, while Jen and I sat there, listening. After a very long while of talking, I finally asked my mom if Jen and I could go in the bedroom and hangout. Luckily, she said yes.

Jen followed me to the other room, and the first thing I said to her was, "So, do you like art?" I have to admit, I was pretty speechless and nervous, so I honestly didn't know what to say.

"Yeah," she replied.

We ended up just sitting on the bed together eating goldfish, (which I spilled many times all over the bed!), and playing on my dad's iPad. Jen said she had one, but left it in her hotel room.

After playing on the iPad, we decided to do Mad Libs. We filled them in with crazy words, and then realized that we were both grammar freaks! After that, we played hide and seek, which didn't work out too well in a tiny hotel room.

When it started to get late we didn't want to leave, so we hid in the closet in the bedroom! We wrote stories together, and we learned that we both liked writing, too. Also, we texted each other with our phones in the closet, which was kinda point-less since we were two feet away from each other.

I used my phone for a flashlight, since it was dark in there. Once I turned the flashlight off, and Jen texted me: "SARAH TODD HAMMER! TURN THE FLASHLIGHT BACK ON!"

We both cracked up.

"Are you mad at me?" Jen asked jokingly.

"I would never be mad at my Jen!" I said in a funny voice.

Soon after that, our parents walked in and jokingly pretended that they couldn't find us.

"Let's go pick up dinner!" they said.

"You have to drive yourself to overcome the obstacles. You might feel that you can't. But then you find your inner strength, and realize you're capable of so much more than you thought."

-Arthur Blank

Jennifer

I was the happiest I'd been in a long time. For hours and hours we talked, played games, and even wrote a silly story! Now we followed our moms to pick up dinner, which ended up being at a Mexican restaurant. We talked the whole walk there and the whole walk back. We never ran out of things to talk about! Looking at our moms, I realized that they weren't running out of conversation subjects either.

When we got back to the hotel the four of us sat down and started eating. American Idol was on, so we watched that during dinner. When the show was over and we ran out of food, we returned to the bedroom to hang out and talk some more.

"Hey, do you usually go by Sarah Todd or Sarah?" I asked kind of randomly.

"Sarah Todd," she responded, and I nodded. That was what I had thought.

We bonded, really bonded, right away, and I never wanted to leave. Time seemed faster, too. When I could have sworn I'd been there for half an hour I looked at the clock and was surprised that it had been 8 hours! I was sure it was the best day of my life. Unfortunately, I had the angiogram just the next day, and I was not excited for that at all.

Sarah Todd

After therapy, my mom and I went back to the hotel. I was very hungry from therapy, so I grabbed a quick snack and watched TV while I ate it. I was so tired from therapy and staying up late the night before with Jen. So, I lied down in my bed and played on my phone. I was thinking about Jen, and wondered how she was doing, since I knew she had some test done. So, I figured that I would send her a quick text message to ask how she was doing.

This was the text conversation between Jen and I:

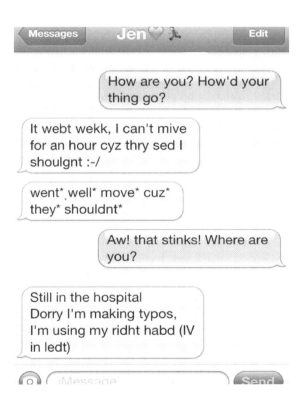

Jennifer

We woke up early for the angiogram the next morning. I texted Sarah Todd really quick, got dressed into comfortable clothes, then went into a taxi with my mom and my grandma, who had arrived to stay with us late the night before. A couple minutes later we were at the Johns Hopkins hospital.

Since I was going under anesthesia I wasn't allowed to eat, so my stomach rumbled. We first went to the heart clinic to get a couple heart tests done, then headed over to start the spinal angiogram. The heart tests were annoying and a little uncomfortable, but not painful or scary. The angiogram, however, terrified me.

A nurse handed me a gown and I quickly tossed it on in the bathroom. I hated hospital gowns, so I tried not to think about it.

Next thing I knew another nurse came in and hooked me up to a heart monitor and an IV, and put a blood pressure cuff on my foot. I lied in a gurney and they wheeled me to the next room, my mom right by my side. When we arrived, they put the anesthesia medicine in my IV. I felt my eyes grow heavy, hearing my mom talking about oceans and the beach as I drifted off.

I woke up with a start. It only took a couple seconds to realize where I was, what I was doing, and that the angiogram was over. I was so glad.

As I drank water, ate Jell-O, and texted some of my friends, a doctor came in. He was really nice! He told me that instead of using reverse medicine they had let me sleep the anesthesia off, because I had to lie down for a couple hours after they were done, anyway. He told me I had about an hour left, and then went on to talking about the results. He said that they hadn't found anything, and these results later led doctors to believe that it either wasn't a spinal cord stroke, or was a mixture of Transverse Myelitis and a spinal cord stroke (started with TM and finished with SCS). This doctor relieved us by saying that either way, it wasn't very likely that I would have a re-occurrence.

We still didn't have exact answers, but at least we were starting to rule things out. Things were starting to fit together like puzzle pieces, and that made me very, very happy.

> "The number of times I succeed is in direct proportion to the number of times I can fail and keep on trying."
>
> - Tom Hopkins

Sarah Todd

Jen and I wanted to meet up again, so we all went to Uno's to have dinner. Jen's grandma Kate came, too! My mom and I took a taxi there, met the Starzecs, and waited for a table. The place was packed! It took forever to finally get a table.

While we waited for our food after we ordered, Jen and I made up Mad Libs for each other, and then some for Kate. We also took pictures together. In one we are both pointing at each other with our tongues sticking out, in another we are smiling, and in one we are acting like we are screaming.

After we were finished eating, we all sat on a bench and talked. None of us wanted to leave each other! We all had had such a great time together.

Jen and I made sure that we traded phone numbers and email addresses before we all said goodbye. After many hugs and goodbyes, my mom and I got in a taxi, and headed back to the hotel.

Jennifer

The next day I had nothing going on, so I begged my mom to try to meet up with Sarah Todd and her mom again. She agreed to talk to them, and Sarah Todd and I started making plans through text. Unfortunately, my right hip hurt really, really bad from the angiogram, so it was hard for me to walk. I didn't want that to get in the way of anything, though.

My mom, grandma and I taxied over to the hospital and headed in, me limping. We asked all over for them to lend us a wheelchair for the day, but could find no one who could let us do that. It was so frustrating. Eventually, we gave up, and rode the subway over to downtown Baltimore to find something to do. I really wanted to go shopping so we went to the mall. Even though I was limping, I still had a great time. I just needed regular breaks. We browsed the clothes, shoes, and makeup, and ended up buying chocolates from Godiva. We ate a small lunch at the food court, and my little blue brace I wore on my right hand fell on the ground, got swept up, and almost thrown away before we noticed. That gave us a laugh!

After shopping some more at the mall we walked over to a restaurant called Uno's for dinner, which was connected to it. My mom texted Sarah Todd's mom as we waited outside the restaurant for a table.

A few minutes later I saw them walking towards us. I was so excited! Our table came, we hung out there, and then some more right outside the restaurant after we were all finished. Although not as much as the hotel room, I ended up having a lot of fun at Uno's, and my hip was temporarily forgotten.

> Never let life's hardships disturb you ... no one can avoid problems,
> not even saints or sages.
> - Nichiren Daishonen

Sarah Todd

Easter was in April, and I love Easter! It's so fun to wake up in the morning and see what's in my Easter basket.

After I got everything out of my basket on Easter of 2012, I grabbed a bucket, and ran outside to hunt for eggs. My mom carried the bucket, and I put the eggs in. There were so many eggs! I got two and a half buckets full!

Buddy came outside and ran around in the backyard. He made a few eggs roll over by pushing them with his nose! My parents and I joked that he was helping me hunt for eggs.

Sometimes my mom or dad would say, "I see one!", and I still couldn't find it! It's funny because after we thought I'd found all of them, we sometimes found some outside after Easter! Even some from a few years before.

I always shook the eggs to see if there was anything inside them. Sometimes there was candy, and other times there were coins.

After a long time of hunting, we thought I was finally finished, because we didn't see any more eggs. I had a really fun time hunting. Also, I got really lucky because Alex and John didn't want to hunt that year, so I got all the eggs!

Jennifer

What was I most excited for once April came around? My first 5k since I got sick, of course! It was at my school, and my whole family and a lot of my friends were running it with me.

The night before the race I set out running clothes, checking and rechecking a million times to make sure I had everything ready. I tossed and turned in bed for hours that night, too, I was so excited!

When morning finally came I threw on the clothes and waited until the rest of my family was ready. We drove over to the school, signed up, and then waited for the race to start.

It started, and everyone started running. I heard my 9-year-old brother cry in pain, and my mom, my mom's cousin Val and I went to check it out. We realized that he had fallen and scraped his knees, which were then bleeding. We waited with him until the principal got help and got him bandaged up.

By now the race had been going for a few minutes, so we started very late. Luckily it wasn't a timed race this year, so it didn't matter that much.

My mom stayed back to go very slow with my injured brother, and Val ran with me to watch me. This was the first time I was running 3.1 miles since August 2011, and I was surprised that my body remembered to fall into a steady, distance pace. I barely felt tired, and that really pleased me! We only stopped briefly to get water at the water station, and that was only at Val's request. She got tired before I did!

Probably about a half hour later we saw the finish line. I sprinted as fast as I could, which was what my body naturally did when the finish line was in sight, leaving Val well behind. Everyone cheered for me. At first, I was a little embarrassed, because I had started late and it looked like I had gone much slower than I had. But then I realized that I had finished a race! I had finished 3.1 miles for the first time since I got TM!

When I got back home, my mom helped me get my running bib off my shirt, and I ran upstairs to add it to my scrapbook. I'd been waiting a long time to start it up again.

"The mind that is anxious about future events is miserable"

- Seneca

Sarah Todd

I finished 4th grade! It was such a great year! All my friends were so sweet, and I had lots of fun. I got an "A" on pretty much every test! I learned so much from my lovely teacher. It was such a joy to have her around!

At lunch my friends and I had never run out of things to talk about, and we laughed and had so much fun together. It was great to get to know my friends all over again. That was the part that I had missed by not being at school the year before: being with my friends.

Then there was Mother's Day. I made my mom her very own board game, and named it, "How Well Do You Know Your Mom?" It was a quiz game with questions about your mom, to see how well you know her! It's a very fun game, and we play it all the time! It was very fun to give it to my mommy. I love her so much!

Jennifer

My school's eighth grade dance was coming up. I was so excited! The year before, in seventh grade, I helped decorate for those eighth graders' dance. I had marveled at how it looked, and couldn't wait until it I got to experience it, too.

Well now it was time. A couple weeks before the dance a couple of my friends, our moms and I went to evening church, dinner, and then dress shopping.

Church and dinner went fine, but by the time I got to the mall I was, annoyingly, in a lot of pain. Luckily, my mom had kept our transport wheelchair, which she had gotten right after my hip troubles in Baltimore in March in case my nerve pains acted up badly again, in the trunk of our car. She put it together in the parking lot really quickly. I sat in it, and my mom wheeled me to the mall.

At the mall my friends Sara and Fabi took turns wheeling me. I think they actually had a little fun with it...

Anyway, we spent many, many hours at the mall trying on dresses to find the perfect one. The people in charge of the dressing rooms kept giving me the largest rooms because of the chair! Also, I got interesting looks from being in a wheelchair through the mall, and I realized how grateful I was to have regained walking while still in the hospital! Being in a wheelchair in a hospital looks normal, but in public people stare. I didn't mind too much that time, but I definitely felt for people with TM who have to use wheelchairs. Well, anybody who has to use a wheelchair for that matter!

Finally, after visiting a million different stores, I found not only the perfect dance dress, but the perfect graduation dress to put under my gown, too!

A couple weeks later was the night I had been waiting for for a long time! It ended up being absolutely perfect, and better than I could ever have imagined.

> "The rose is fairest when 'tis is budding new,
> and hope is brightest when it dawns from fears"
> - Walter Scott

Sarah Todd

Summertime was here! I was so happy. Warm weather is the best. It's shorts weather, and the perfect time to be outside. Plus, when it's warm, my hands don't freeze up, so I can move my right hand freely. Also, we could now finally use our pool! It was so nice! We had been waiting a long time to try it out. It was so warm. I absolutely loved it.

I also looked forward to going on Gran and Grandad's beach trip with my Uncle Nat, Uncle Steve, Auntie Robynne, Auntie Kelly, and my cousins Michael, Chris, Andrew, and Katie. We had missed the last few years so I was excited to go. Thank goodness I have a girl cousin to hang out with! We go to Myrtle Beach, South Carolina and we each get condos right next to each other. That way, we can visit with each other more, since we're near each other. We used to all stay in one big beach house together, but we stopped doing that a few years before.

Summer is the best time in the world. No school, warm weather, and hanging out with friends. I was happy it was finally here.

"Every moment and every event of every man's life on Earth plants
something in his soul."

- Thomas Merton

Jennifer

My eighth grade year was now officially over.

On June fourth, 2012 the school day was filled with special events. For
lunch we went outside for the eighth grade picnic. The air was perfect picnic weather:
warm but not too hot, and not too windy.

After the picnic was the awards ceremony. The first award they gave out was
one that I won! It was a really special award, called the American Legion award.
When they called my name I walked onto the stage, and a man handed me a certificate, a check for $50, and a ribbon. He then proceeded to say very nice, good things
about me. It was an incredible experience!

That wasn't the first time I had won an award that year. The other time started at the beginning of the school year, when we wrote essays in English class to send
to the Grayslake Exchange Club. The essays were mostly about accomplishments
and hardships throughout our lives. I wrote a lot about TM, which was a little nerve-
wracking because it was the first time I was being so open about it. But in the end, I
was glad I did, because it made a very good essay. I was one of the winners! I found
that out and had gotten the award in March.

Both awards together made for a great end to my eighth grade year.

"Jennifer M. Starzec"

I heard my name being called from backstage that evening, dressed in my
long blue graduation robe. I walked across the stage in a daze, simultaneously reach-
ing out with my very weak right hand to shake my principal's hand and taking my
diploma from him with my left hand when I got to him.

"Good job, Jennifer," he whispered.

> "The only journey is the journey within"
> - Rainer Maria Rilke

Sarah Todd

I realize today that this is the hand I've been dealt, the life I've been given. If I could change one thing about my life, I wouldn't. The opportunities that I have today, and where I am, are incredible. Everyone I've met throughout this experience, I wouldn't know today if Transverse Myelitis didn't come into my life. Everything happens for a reason, and God will give you that reason.

"All the world is full of suffering. It is also full of overcoming"

-Helen Keller

Jennifer

Today, I look throughout the scrapbook I created for my races back when I started running. I flip through the pages, looking at the numbers on each bib I glued in there, and letting the words on the certificate I received for cross country in seventh grade embed themselves in my mind.

I stop myself at one of the last pages. The heading reads, "Just Book It; August 6th, 2011". I look at the number, and see a short message written on the side of the bib.

"To Jennifer, my best wishes."

-Tom O'Hara

"There is no happiness except in the realization that we have accomplished

something"

-Henry Ford

Epilogue

As you may have noticed while reading Jennifer and Sarah Todd's journey, both girls have recovered greatly since the onset of their Transverse Myelitis. However, there are still symptoms and effects affecting them today.

Currently Jen's biggest issues are chronic nerve pain and fatigue. Other things affecting her are low bone density, random blurred vision episodes, muscle atrophy, partial paralysis in the right shoulder/forearm/hand, weakness in the left hand, and scoliosis.

Currently, Sarah Todd's biggest issue is paralysis. She has had very limited regain in movement in both of her shoulders, arms, and hands. She also is not able to move her left fingers at all and has limited use of her right hand. Like Jen, she also has other medical issues affecting her, including scoliosis, muscle atrophy, and low bone density.

Pictures

You read our journey... Now you get to walk through it with pictures!

Sarah Todd: Me at my very first piano recital on April 17th, 2010, two days before I got TM.

Jen: A few months before I got Transverse Myelitis, after running the Frosty Foot Race. I got second place in my age group.

Events From Part 1

Jen: On the left is when the therapy dog came to visit in the hospital. The lady helped me pet the dog by moving my hand for me. On the right is me able to sit up in the hospital.

Sarah Todd: On the left is the music therapist in the hospital playing guitar while I sing "You Belong With Me". On the right is the beautiful "Welcome Home" sign that my friends and neighbors worked hard to make.

Events From Part 2

Jen: On the left is me trying to ride the arm bike at therapy. On the right is a few friends and I holding posters we made for our moms when they ran the Chicago marathon (I'm in the front on the far right with the infamous Prednisone moon face… yuck!).

Sarah Todd: On the left is my Cinderella costume Katie made me for Halloween in 2011. On the right is me riding a horse at Victory Junction.

Events From Part 3

Sarah Todd: On the left is me standing with my 4th grade science fair project in the school gym. On the right is my mom and I after I gave her the special board game I made her.

Jen: On the left is me receiving my award at my eighth grade awards ceremony. On the right is my running bib from the "Just Book It" race, which former Olympic runner Tom O'Hara signed just ten days before TM.

Acknowledgements

First, we would like to give a HUGE thanks to OUR PARENTS!

Mommy and Daddy, I love you so much and I want to thank you for always being there for me. You have helped me make it through a lot, and I wouldn't be where I am right now without you. I don't know what I would do without you in my life. I love you with all my heart!
- Sarah Todd

Momma and Daddy, there is no way I would have made it this far without you guys. You guys did all you could to help me get through everything, good and bad! You are my biggest supporters, and I don't know what I would have done without you. I love you!
- Jen

We would also like to thank the rest of our family and all of our friends. Thank you for continuing to support us! We love you!

Finally, we would like to give a special thanks to Umaiyal Sridas for making the cover. Thanks, Umaiyal! Our book wouldn't look as pretty without you!

About The Authors

Jennifer Starzec is 15 years old and has had Transverse Myelitis for almost 2 years. She enjoys writing, reading, and, most of all, running. Her best three mile time since

she got sick (or in her life, for that matter) as of now is 22 minutes and 45 seconds. She lives in Illinois with her mom, dad, four brothers (Reese, Harrison, Tristan, and Bryce), and one sister (Jolie). This is her second published book; she is also the author of the children's book *Benny the Runt Banana*.

Sarah Todd Hammer is 11 years old, and is in 6th grade. She has had Transverse Myelitis for about 3 years. She lives in Atlanta, GA with her Mom, Dad, and two older brothers (Alex and John). Sarah Todd's most favorite hobbies are dancing, choreographing, singing, and writing. She has choreographed dances to Carrie Underwood's songs "That's Where It Is" and "Some Hearts". She enjoys watching Dance Moms, and makes up dances to songs from the show. This is Sarah Todd's first ever published book.